ISBN 0-446-34766-3

>>$4.95<<

A Few Minutes *with* Andy Rooney

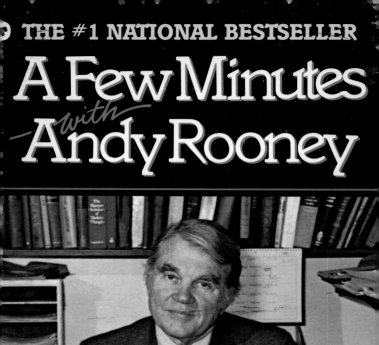

by ANDREW A. ROONEY

THEY'RE ALL RAVING ABOUT
ANDY ROONEY... LISTEN:

MIKE WALLACE — "Andy Rooney has been watching us all, you and me, for years and years, and finally he decided to tell us what he's found out. He's perceptive and wise, but most of all he's funny."

FRED GRAHAM — "Andy Rooney is either the smartest funny man or the funniest smart man I have ever known. I know that his book will make people laugh—and think—about things they otherwise wouldn't have noticed."

ROBERT MacNEIL — "Andy Rooney is one of the few really funny men in a society that takes itself too seriously by half."

CHARLES OSGOOD — "There is nothing common about common sense. That's why there is only one Andy Rooney...in the strictest sense, inimitable."

JIM LEHRER — "He's one of us. His soap is slippery, too; his mailbox is full of junk mail, too. He understands."

BILL MOYERS — "Rumors of Mark Twain's demise were indeed exaggerated; he is alive and well and appearing regularly on *60 Minutes*."

FRED W. FRIENDLY — *"A Few Minutes With Andy Rooney* is a vital trip to the thinking man's amusement park."

GARSON KANIN — "A unique and original American humorist in the hilarious tradition of Twain, Ade, Dunne, Rogers, Benchley, Thurber and Perelman."

Books by
ANDREW A. ROONEY

A Few Minutes
With Andy Rooney

And More By Andy Rooney

Published by
WARNER BOOKS

A Few Minutes with Andy Rooney

by ANDREW A. ROONEY

WARNER BOOKS

A Warner Communications Company

WARNER BOOKS EDITION

This Warner Books Edition is published by arrangement with Atheneum Publishers, 597 Fifth Avenue, New York, N.Y. 10017

Cover photographed by Irving Haberman
Cover design copyright © 1981 by Mike Stromberg.

Warner Books, Inc.
666 Fifth Avenue
New York, N.Y. 10103

Ⓦ A Warner Communications Company

Printed in the United States of America

First Warner Books Printing: *December, 1982*

10 9

CONTENTS

Ourselves

PREFACE

The writing in this book was originally done for television. S.J. Perelman said the only difference in writing for television is that to make it look like a script, you only write on the right-hand side of the paper. There are other differences, though.

Words written for television are meant to be heard by the ear, not seen by the eye. People don't talk the way they write and they don't write the way they talk, so you have to make some adjustments. When a writer puts it down on paper, he's more concise than he'd be in conversation. He cuts out a lot of the hemming and hawing and backtracking that all of us do when we talk. This saves everyone time but the writer. He thinks out what he's going to say in advance and then tries to stick to the point.

When the same writer puts words down to be spoken by someone on television, on a stage or in a motion picture, he puts a little of the hemming and hawing back in to make it sound more natural. At best it comes out as a compromise between written and spoken English.

To be spoken aloud, the sentences have to be shorter and the writing simpler. You can't turn a clever phrase because if the audience doesn't catch it the first time, they can't go back and read it over again. At the same time, a viewer or listener expects more from something that's been written to be said than he'd expect to hear from a friend he meets on the street, so the writing has to be a little concentrated.

If it is concentrated and there are ideas in the writing, it has to be slowed down because all of us talk faster than we listen. Writing for television, you often follow an idea with a few words that don't mean much just to give listeners time to hear what you've said.

If I were teaching a class of young writers, I'd advise them to keep in mind what something sounds like when they read it aloud, even if what they are writing is for print. Anyone should be very suspicious of a sentence he's written that can't be read aloud easily.

I'm telling you all this because I assume that if you weren't interested you wouldn't have bought the book. I hope it's a good book. Publishers these days are often more interested in whether something will sell than whether it's any good. A book by anyone on a popular television broadcast will probably sell whether it's any good or not and that makes me nervous.

It wasn't hard to talk me into putting this book together. It is unsatisfactory for a writer to have his words said once and then disappear forever into thin air. Seeing our names in print leads to the dream all of us have of immortality. You can't ask more from something than immortality and money next week.

I use the phrase "putting this book together" because it's been written over a period of ten years. For print I've crossed out some things that don't mean anything at all without the pictures that originally went with them, and I've put apostrophes back in words like "*Ive*," "*dont*" and "*isnt*" which *Ive* abandoned in writing for television. For the most part, though, these essays are printed as broadcast.

The writer doesn't have much stature in the visual arts and, being as I am a writer, that irritates me. The performers and the producers get more of everything than the creators in most cases. Television writing in particular has been considered a second-class art form and that's why so much of it isn't any good. Almost none of the good writers who have already established themselves in print have turned to television. This is part television's fault for not encouraging them and part their own fault. Some of them are afraid they don't know how to do it and they hesitate to risk their reputations trying.

Even within the television industry, writers tend to leave their work to become producers as if that was a higher calling. (I don't use the subjunctive much writing for television.) They get more power, more money and they no longer have to make fools of themselves putting it down on paper where everyone can see it.

If the normal law of supply and demand worked, there would be a lot more writers than there are. There are hundreds of producers, directors, publishers, editors, actors and salesmen waiting for one writer to put something down on paper so they can change it, duplicate it and sell it. Hollywood and Broadway—and television in both places— are desperately in need of good writers. There are enough actors looking for work today to do all the plays, television productions and movies that will be written for the next fifty years.

Nonfiction writing in television is almost nonexistent outside the hard-news area. Even though more than half the best-selling books and mass-circulation magazines are nonfiction, commercial television has never given it much of a chance because network executives don't think it will attract a crowd. They are wrong and they'll change their minds.

You don't know Bob Forte and Jane Bradford but the three of us have worked together for ten years. They are important to the things I've done, and I'd feel terrible if their names weren't somewhere in this book.

Now I want to check my dictionary to see whether this is a preface, a foreword or an introduction.

ANDREW A. ROONEY

Belongings

CHAIRS

There is so much that is unpleasant and dull about living that we ought to take every opportunity presented to us to enjoy the enjoyable things in life. None of us can afford to become immune to the sensation of small pleasures or uninterested in small interests. A chair, for instance, can be a small and constant joy, and taking pleasure from one a sensation available to almost all of us all the time.

It is relatively easy to say who invented the light bulb but impossible to say who built the first chair. They took one out of King Tut's tomb when they opened it in 1922 and King Tut died fourteen hundred years before Christ was born and that certainly wasn't the first chair, either. So they've been around a long time. If there was a first man, he probably sat in the first chair.

Chairs have always been something more than a place for us to bend in the middle and put our posteriors on other legs in order to take the weight off our own. They have been a symbol of power and authority, probably because before the sixteenth century only the very rich *owned* real chairs. The others sat on the floor at their feet in most countries.

A throne is the ultimate place to sit down and there are still something like twenty-five countries in the world that have thrones, and leaders who actually sit on them.

The Peacock Throne of Persia is one of the most elaborate, but I don't know what happened to that. It belonged to the King of Persia, but Persia is called Iran now and, of course, they don't have a king. The leaders they have now usually sit on the floor. I suppose this is their way of reacting against the idiocy of a throne but I hope they haven't discarded theirs. It was crusted with rubies and diamonds and was supposed to be worth $100 million twenty years ago. In today's market I should think it would bring $500 million, although I don't know who it would bring it from.

I've seen pictures of it but, personally, I wouldn't give them $50 million for it, and if the average American housewife got hold of it, she'd probably put a slipcover over it.

I didn't mean to get off on thrones but some kings and queens have more than one. Queen Elizabeth has one in every Commonwealth country, presumably in the event she wants to sit down if she visits one of them. She has five in London alone and several more at palaces around England. I'd hate to have to reglue a throne.

If the United States had a king, I suppose there'd be a throne in the White House. Too bad there isn't, in a way. It could be more of a tourist attraction than the Washington Monument.

Theoretically the royal chair is never sat in by anyone but a nation's ruler, but it's hard to believe that a few of the cleaning ladies and some of the kids around the castle don't test it out once in a while. I can imagine the guards in a state

4

prison fooling around in the electric chair, too. "Hey, Joe. Look at me. Throw the switch!"

The closest thing we ever had to a throne was that big rocking chair John Kennedy intimidated people with. A visiting dignitary could be disarmed by its folksy charm and overwhelmed by its size and mobility.

There's nothing else like chairs that we have in such great numbers. We know how many cars there are in this country and how many television sets, but we don't have the vaguest idea how many chairs there are. I'll bet if everyone sat down in one, there'd still be fifty empty chairs left over for each one of us.

Over the past fifty years the most used piece of furniture in the house has been the kitchen chair. Like anything that gains wide acceptance, it turns out to be useful for a lot of things it wasn't built to do. The kitchen chair is for sitting on, for throwing clothes over, for hanging jackets on, for putting a foot on when you're lacing a shoe, and as an all-purpose stepladder for changing light bulbs or for getting down infrequently used dishes from high and remote parts of kitchen cabinets. It has usually been painted many times, hurriedly.

If the kitchen chair isn't the most sat on, the one the American working man comes home to every evening must be. (The American working woman doesn't have a chair of her own.) It's the one in which he slumps for endless hours watching football games on television. It's the one in which he is portrayed in cartoons about himself and it's usually the most comfortable chair in the house. It's a chair you sit in, not on.

It isn't so much that the American male takes this throne as his prerogative. It's that women don't usually like a chair that mushy. It's a comfortable chair, though, and for all its gross, overfed appearance, I'm not knocking it. It serves as a bed when it's too early to go to bed. It's a place where you can take a nap before turning in for a night's sleep.

In big cities you see a lot of overstuffed chairs being thrown away outside apartment houses. I always think of the old Eskimo women they put out on an ice floe to die.

The kitchen chair and the overstuffed living-room chair are

the *most* sat on, and there are always a few chairs in every home that no one ever sits on. Everyone in the household understands about it. There are no rules. It is just not a chair you sit on. It may be in the hall by the front door, used mostly for piling books on after school. Or it may be silk brocade with a gold fringe, in the back bedroom. It may be antique and uncomfortable or imperfectly glued together and therefore too fragile for the wear-and-tear that goes with being sat on regularly.

Sometimes there is no reason that anyone can give why a chair isn't sat on. It's like the suit or dress in the closet which is perfectly good but never worn. The unsat-upon chair in a home really isn't much good for anything except handing down from one generation to the next.

In hotels they often put two chairs not to be sat in on either side of the mirror across from the elevator on every floor.

There aren't as many dining-room chairs as there used to be because there aren't as many dining rooms. Now people eat in the kitchen or they have picnics in front of the television set in the living room. It's too bad, because there's something civilized and charming about having a special place for eating. It's a disappearing luxury, though. These days everything in a house has to be multipurpose, folding, retractable or convertible.

Dining-room chairs on thick rugs were always a problem. They made it difficult or impossible for a polite man to slide a chair under a woman. As soon as any of her weight fell on the chair, the legs sank into the pile and stopped sliding. If she was still eight inches from where she wanted to be, she had to put her hands under the seat and hump it toward the table while the man made some futile gestures toward helping from behind her. It took a lot of the grace out of the gesture.

The other trouble with a good set of dining-room chairs was that at Christmas or any other special occasion when you

wanted them most, there weren't enough of them. This meant bringing a chair or two in from the kitchen or the living room and ruining the effect of a matched set.

If dining-room chairs are the most gracious, folding chairs are the least. I suppose someone will collect those basic folding, wood chairs they kept in church basements and sell them as antiques someday soon, but they're ugly and uncomfortable. Maybe they were designed to keep people awake at town meetings.

The Morris chair was invented by an English poet named William Morris. He's better known for his chair than his poetry. A man takes immortality from anywhere he can get it, but it seems a sad fate for a poet to be remembered for a chair. I make furniture myself and I hate to think of any table I've made outlasting my writing, but I suppose it could happen.

Very few chairs survive the age in which they were designed. The Windsor chair is one of a handful of classics that have. The Hitchcock is another. If the time comes when we want to place a time capsule to show people on another planet in another eon what we sat on, we should put a Windsor chair in to represent us. You have to choose something better than average as typical.

The rocking chair probably comes closer than any other article of furniture to delineating past generations from present ones. People sat in them and contemplated their lives and the lives of people they could see passing by from where they sat. People don't contemplate each other much from chairs anymore. When anyone passes by now, he's in a car going too fast for anyone to identify him. No one is sitting on the front porch watching from a rocker anyway.

Rockers were good furniture. They were comfortable and gave the user an air of ease and contentment. They give the person sitting in one the impression he's getting somewhere without adding any of the headaches that come with progress.

From time to time furniture makers say there's a revived interest in rocking chairs, but I doubt this. For one thing, the front porch has probably been closed in to make the living room bigger and anyway people don't want anything as mobile or folksy as a rocker in a living room filled with electronic gear.

Comfort in a chair is often in direct ratio to the relationship between the height of the feet and the height of the head. People are always trying to get their feet up. Very likely there is an instinct for self-preservation here because the closer anyone's feet are to being on a level with the head, the less work the heart has to do to get the blood pumped around.

During the years between World War I and World War II, everyone's dream of a vacation was a boat trip somewhere on the *Mauretania*, the *Leviathan* or one of the *Queens* to Europe. In their dreams, the man and the woman were stretched out in the bright sunshine on deck chairs in mid-Atlantic. Not many people go by boat anywhere anymore, though, and the deck or steamer chairs were redesigned and moved to the backyard. The wood in those deck chairs has been replaced by tubular aluminum and the canvas by plastic straps. They wouldn't have lasted five minutes on the deck of the *Mauretania* in a stiff breeze.

At some time in the last hundred years, we reached the point where more people were working sitting down than on their feet. This could be a milestone unturned by social historians. We have more and more white-collar people and executives sitting in chairs telling people what to do and fewer and fewer people on their feet actually doing anything.

The sitting executives found that they weren't satisfied not moving at all, so they invented a chair for executives that swivels, rolls forward, backward or sideways and tilts back when the executive, who used to have his feet on the ground, wants to lean back and put them on his mahogany desk.

In many offices the chairs provided for men and for women are symbols that irritate progressive women. The chairs often represent clear distinctions in the relative power of the sexes there. The executive male has his bottom on a cushion, his elbows on armrests. At the desk outside his office, the secretary, invariably a woman, sits erect in a typing chair about as comfortable as an English saddle.

It's a strange thing and probably says a lot about our rush through life that the word "modern" has an old-fashioned connotation to it when you're talking about design. I think of Art Deco as modern. It must be because what we call "modern" is just a brand-new design about to become

obsolete. Someone is always coming up with what is known as a modern chair. It looks old and silly in a few years but is still referred to as modern.

There are modern chairs that have not become obsolete because they're so good. Some of them are forty years old but they're still called modern. Charles Eames designed that plastic bucket seat on tubular legs that will not go out of style. Mies van der Rohe designed the Barcelona chair that you have in the outer lobby of your office if you're a rich company. That's going to last like the Windsor and the Boston rockers because it's comfortable and simply attractive.

Considering how much time we spend sitting, it's strange

our chairs don't fit us better. No size 6 woman would think of wearing a size 14 dress but a size 48 man who weighs 250 pounds is expected to sit in the same size chair a 98-pound woman sits in. To some extent a chair in a room is considered community property, but in most homes a family arranges itself in the same way day after day when it settles down, and more attention ought to be given chair sizes.

Certain purposeful chairs have been well done but with no regard to the size or shape of the occupant. The electric chair, the dentist's chair, the theater seat or the airplane seat are mostly well designed, but again every chair is the same size. We're not. I suppose it would be difficult to sell theater tickets by seat size or for a dentist to have more than one chair depending on whose tooth ached. But the fact remains: people don't take the same size chair any more than they take the same size shoe.

Even though most public seating furniture must have seemed comfortable to the people who designed it, it seems to have been designed and sat on for the test under laboratory conditions. These conditions don't exist in a movie theater or on a crowded airplane.

In the theater chair, the shared armrest has always been a problem. The dominant personality usually ends up using the one on both sides of the seat in which he or she is sitting and the occupants of the adjacent seats get either none or one, depending on who flanks them on the *other* side. The shared armrest may be part of what's known as the magic of the theater, but it's a constant source of irritation to anyone watching a bad movie.

The average airplane chair is a marvel of comfort and we could all do worse than to have several installed in our own homes. The problem on board, of course, is the person in the seat next to you. The seats are usually lined up three across, and if the plane is full the middle seat can make a trip to

Europe a nightmare. It is no longer a comfortable place of repose; it's a trap and you're in it.

At a time when all of us are looking for clues to our character, it's unusual that no one has started analyzing us from the way we sit in chairs. It must be at least as revealing of character as a person's handwriting and an even more reliable indicator of both personality and attitude than, say, palm-reading.

The first few minutes after you sit down are satisfying ones, but no matter how good it feels to get off your feet, you can't stay in one position very long. Sooner or later that wonderful feeling you got when you first took the weight off your feet goes away. You begin to twitch. You are somehow dissatisfied with the way your body is arranged in the chair but uncertain as to what to do about it.

Everyone finds his own solution for what to do with feet. No two people do exactly the same thing. The first major alteration in the sitting position usually comes when the legs are crossed. The crossing of legs seems to satisfy some inner discontent, the scratching of a psychosomatic itch deep inside.

It's amusing to see how often we use a chair designed to be used one way in a manner so totally different that even the originator could not have imagined it. We straddle a chair, sitting on it backwards with our arms where our backs are supposed to be and our chin on our arms; we sit sideways in a lounge chair with our legs draped over one arm and our backs leaning against the other arm. We rock back in chairs that are not rockers, ungluing their joints. We do things to chairs we wouldn't do to our worst enemy, and chairs are among our best friends.

You'd have to say that of all the things we have built for ourselves to make life on earth more tolerable, the chair has been one of the most successful.

WHO OWNS WHAT
IN AMERICA

We used to toast Pepperidge Farm bread for breakfast in my house; then the little company that made it was taken over by Campbell Soup, a big company, and I don't think the bread's as good as it used to be.

Whenever a big company takes over a small company, the product almost always gets worse. Sue me, but it's true. The takeover is so popular with big business it's hard to know who owns what in America.

Take, for example, the International Telephone and Telegraph Company. They do some telephone business, I guess, but they also own Sheraton Hotels, the Hartford Fire Insurance Company, the company that publishes *Who's Who in America* and the bakeries that make Hostess Twinkies.

Most of the tobacco companies have taken over so many other companies that they've dropped "tobacco" from their names. Philip Morris bought that fine old German beer

Lowenbrau, which they now make in such fine old German cities as Fort Worth, Texas. Liggett, known for its Chesterfield cigarettes, owns J & B Scotch and the company that makes Champion barbells. The former Reynolds Tobacco Company owns Chun King foods, Hawaiian Punch and Vermont Maid syrup, which is 2% maple and not made in Vermont.

Who would you think owns Montgomery Ward? Sears, Roebuck? Wrong. Mobil Oil owns Montgomery Ward.

Pepsi-Cola owns Wilson, which makes tennis balls. And don't try to find a Coca-Cola in a Pizza Hut because Pepsi-Cola owns them, too.

General Mills, which bought Bruce Jenner, the champion of breakfasts, owns Lacoste, the company that makes the tennis shirt with the little alligator on it. General Mills also owns the game of Monopoly.

Hershey makes chocolate bars, but also owns the San Giorgio Macaroni Company.

Consolidated Foods makes Sara Lee cheesecake, which seems fitting, and Electrolux vacuum cleaners, which doesn't.

ABC, Number 1 in television, owns *Prairie Farmer* magazine, but CBS isn't worried. It owns *Field & Stream* and *Woman's Day.*

Recently the Kellogg Company paid $56 million for a company called Mrs. Smith's Pies.

Big companies love homey-sounding little names like Mrs. Smith's Pies. We decided to go to Pottstown, Pennsylvania, where the pies are made, to see if we could find out what Mrs. Smith is going to do with the $56 million.

ROONEY:
Pardon me, do you know where Mrs. Smith is?
MAN:
Mrs. Smith?
ROONEY:
Yeah.

MAN:

What Mrs. Smith is that?

WOMAN:

Right. No, look, go here to the end of the alley and make a right.

ROONEY:

Where's the main office, do you know? Will Mrs. Smith be there?

MAN:

A Mr. Smith?

ROONEY:

No, *Mrs*. Smith. Is it *Mr*. Smith's Pies?

ROONEY:

Hi. You're Mrs. Smith, are you?

WOMAN:

No, I'm not.

ROONEY (in factory parking lot):

Is there a Mrs. Smith? Smith isn't around at all?

MAN:

No, there's a . . . there's no Smiths connected with the company at this time. It's owned by Kellogg's.

Who owns what in America? Not Mrs. Smith.

SOAP

I went out and bought as many bars and cakes of soap as I could find in the local stores around me. Americans buy about two billion of them a year—eight or ten cakes for each one of us. I've been to a couple of countries where I doubt the whole population uses eight or ten cakes a year. Nasty American thing to say, isn't it?

The most expensive one I found was Bronnley. It's soap in a little sponge pillow. It was $7.50. I can't wait until I submit an expense account and the money people at CBS see this: one cake of soap—$7.50.

Chanel No. 5. Hand soap, it says. Wouldn't want to get any of it on your face, I guess.

Guerlain's. They make perfume, too. I don't like perfumed soap. Soap, like people, shouldn't smell like anything. If soap smells too much, I figure they're hiding something.

A lot of the expensive ones sound like something to eat. Milk 'n Honey—contains milk proteins and pure honey. You wouldn't want to wash up with impure honey. Oatmeal.

Victorian Herb soap—soap or soup? Soap—made of lettuce juice, it says. "Lettuce juice is calmative to rough skin." This one "combines the natural smoothness of avocado with the goodness of honey." Cucumber & Glycerine. I guess of all the things I'd least want to wash up with, it would be cucumber. Here's one that looks like a lemon. Cocoa Butter. Pears. I know Pears. It's transparent—in case you want to see through your soap. I suppose if you were washing someone else's back.

These are all the exotic soaps, of course, the expensive ones, that not many of us use. They're too expensive for us. The ones most of us use are Dial, Lux, Camay, Dove, Palmolive. I don't know which the best-seller is.

I don't have much complaint with American soaps—any one of them. Oh, I have a few complaints. For one thing, most of its lifetime a cake of soap is too small. I brought one in from the house. It's not a cake at all. It's more like a thin cookie. It's not only too small, it's sharp around the edges. No one wants sharp soap. The fact is a cake of soap is only at its best for two or three days, while you can still feel the letters on it. I'd like to be rich enough to throw soap away after the letters are worn off.

A lot of these are different colors, too. They're green and brown. Soap should be white. Dishes, underwear and soap should all be white. When a person takes a shower and looks down, he doesn't want to see a lot of colors running off him.

And just one last comment. Are the soap manufacturers paying off the people who build soap dishes into showers? If they aren't, how come the soap holders are always placed so they take a direct hit from the shower water; then, for the rest of the day the soap just sits there dissolving in a puddle of water?

And how about slippery, too, you soapmakers? You make it slippery on purpose so we'll drop it in the water, don't you? Huh?

JEANS

All blue jeans were ever meant to be were comfortable pants to work in or hang around the house in, Saturday morning. What in the world has happened to blue jeans?

Do we really have to go to Paris to get a pair of blue denim pants designed—two legs, a fly and some belt loops? Who is this Sergio Valente, anyway, and what's he done with pants that's so different?

I don't understand it. Everywhere you go these days, you're faced with the rear end of some pretty model posing in some unlikely position, trying to sell you blue jeans. They're on the backs of the buses everywhere . . . although I shouldn't think anyone who could pay for Jou Jou jeans would *take* a bus.

The ads stare down at you from billboards all over town. He loves her pants. She loves his pants. There's an awful lot of panting going on in these jean ads.

23

How come they wear so much below the waist and so little above it in some of the ads? I should think they'd get cold.

Oh, I think I know *why* they don't wear much. It's because one pair of blue jeans looks so much like the next pair of blue jeans that the designer's trying to take our eyes off the pants by attracting us to look elsewhere.

Now even the old-time jean makers like Levi and Wrangler have put fly fronts on women's pants and they're going for the designer market, too. To hear the women talk—often upside down—in the television commercials, you'd think all they want in the *whole world* is a new pair of pants.

I don't care how the pants look upside down. What I want to know is: How do they look after they've been in a heap on the floor all night?

Most designers put their names on the back of the jeans somewhere. Gloria Vanderbilt or Calvin Klein are status symbols pinned to your tail. Frankly, I wouldn't want Gloria's name on my tail, and I'm surprised she'd want it there either.

There's no doubt all this advertising has sold a lot of blue jeans. You see them on the street everywhere. They've taken over from khaki and corduroy. Some blue jeans aren't even blue anymore. But if you look at the people wearing them in the streets, one problem is apparent: most Americans simply do not have the designers' ideal derrière. If all the women in America were built like jean models, it would be different. But the promises of the advertising greatly exceed the fact of the average American posterior.

Just an opinion.

WARRANTIES

What do you do with all the owner's manuals, warranties and pieces of paper that come in the box when you buy something new? I never know what to do with them.

I bought a new blender last week and there were eight separate things to read in there. I'm having a good time opening my new toy and the first thing I get is a warning: "STOP!" They don't want me to hurt myself. "To avoid injury," it says, "see your recipe book for assembly instructions."

Well, in the first place, I didn't know I had to put the thing together myself, and in the second place, why would they put the assembly instructions in the *recipe* book?

"Place stamp here!" That's something I'm supposed to mail back to them if something is missing. Why didn't *they* make sure nothing is missing? If I have to put something together myself, I *always* think something's missing.

Here's the important one: "Owner's registration card."

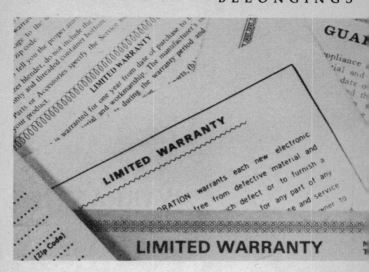

LIMITED WARRANTY

They want your name, address, date of birth, color of eyes, where you bought it, why you bought it and how you paid for it. It's as if they thought you *stole* it.

"IMPORTANT DO NOT DESTROY!" See, that's why I don't dare throw any of this out . . . they tell me not to.

I dug up all the guarantees I found in drawers around the house. I've got more old warranty cards than drawers to put them in. Let's face it, though, anything that's apt to happen to an appliance like a blender isn't covered by the warranty anyway, so I never send them in. If it breaks, I'll buy a new one. That's the American way.

"Congratulations, you are now the proud owner of a new GE automatic slicer. With care it will give many years of faithful service." They all say the same things. It doesn't matter whether you buy a radio, a power tool or a new refrigerator. You know:

"Read instructions carefully."

"Do not immerse in water."

"Keep out of the reach of children."

"Wash occasionally in a mild solution of soap and warm water."

I've got one for an automatic dryer. We threw the dryer away nine years ago, but I'm still holding on to the warranty and the owner's manual.

"Your new drill is an outstanding value, combining quality with versatility." They keep selling you on these things even after they've got your money. "Made from the finest materials available."

They usually promise these things won't break, too, but I notice they always include a list of places where you can get them fixed. Montana, North Dakota . . . there's never a place near me.

"If this item has to be returned, mail it back in its original container." They're kidding. They expect us to save all that stuff too? I'd have to take it all back to Japan to find someone who could put it back in the package it came in.

And one last bit of reading matter: "Batteries not included."

DIRECTIONS

Do you find it hard to follow directions?

I was thinking of installing one of those automatic garage-door openers over the weekend. The directions say, "Make certain the garage door is square and straight and that the garage floor is level." Directions always read like that.

Is everything in your house straight, square and level? If my house was straight, square and level, I would never have to fix anything. What we all need are directions that tell us what to do when everything is crooked, off-center and all screwed up.

You buy a can of paint. You get ready to go to work. The paint seems a little thick, so you read the directions between the drips running down the side of the can. It says, "Make certain the surface is absolutely free of dirt, dust, grease or rust."

If the surface was perfect, would I be painting it?

The recipe in the newspaper gives you directions. They say, "Have your butcher prepare three six-ounce pheasants."

What butcher? All I ever see is a lot of packaged meat in the refrigerator counter, with the fat and the bones hidden on the downside. I don't have a butcher any more than I have a straight, square and level house.

You call the airlines. Ticket-seller takes the information and then gives you directions. Says, "Be at the airport to pick up your ticket at least an hour before flight time."

Well, if I have to be out at the airport an hour in advance, I might as well take the *bus* from downtown to where I'm going.

Then I like the directions we get from those consumer-affairs people about how to handle these problems. "If you want to get your car repaired," they tell you, "get at least three estimates in writing."

Have you ever taken your car to a garage without knowing what's wrong with it and demanded a written estimate from the mechanic on how much he'll charge to fix it?

If the pain persists, see your doctor.

CATALOGS

Do you read the catalogs the stores send to your home?

The women's catalogs are the best. I love how natural-looking the models are. Just plain folks, aren't they? They could be the girl next door, right? Miss Average American Woman.

They put the models in such everyday settings, too. They're always perching them on rocks somewhere. It's something you see all the time, isn't it: three women in the back of a covered wagon in decorator-designed underwear?

"The mark of Halston is graceful simplicity." The model stands there in a graceful, simple pose. You wonder how long she could hold it without dropping dead.

I like the writing, too. Women's clothes are always "versatile." They do "double duty." A pair of tweed knickers can be turned upside down and made into a downy-soft wraparound for poolside, according to the advertisements. An

evening gown converts into a sleeping bag or a poncho or maybe a mountain-climbing ensemble.

"Eggplant polyester": this is a color? They never use the names of any real colors in these women's catalogs. They never use red, for instance. Everything's either claret or burgundy. They're always inventing new names for colors: "cranberry," "nutmeg," "sea foam," "celery," "cinnamon," "taupe"—whatever taupe is—"stone," "brick." You know: fine, but what color is it?

"Hugs the body." I don't know about you but I don't want clothes hugging my body. I like to leave some doubt about where my clothes end and my body begins.

The men in these catalogs all look a lot like me, I think. They're handsome, young, rugged, about 150 pounds and never a hair out of place. I relate to these guys; this is what we look like hanging around the house watching television in a velvet lounge ensemble. Just perfect. Even if we're wearing overalls, we look as though we've just been dusted.

You notice the male models in the pictures usually only put four fingers in their pockets, too. They leave their thumbs out. I don't know what that does for them.

I like the gadget catalogs, too. They always have just what you need . . . cordless electric pepper mills, things like that. Whatever it is, you just set it and forget it. "No more muss . . . no more fuss."

And I like the folksy catalogs. They often have the picture of the company's president and founder in them.

"Our president has searched the world over to bring you this rugged, three-speed, reversible, glen-plaid eggbeater. Never needs oiling."

I love looking through all these catalogs. And just one more thing: "Please allow six to eight weeks for delivery."

SIZES

It seems to me we're mixed up about the way we designate the size of things.

Look at the boxes of soap flakes, for example. Which size would you think was bigger: the jumbo, the giant, or the king size? The king size looks bigger, but it turns out that the jumbo box weighs nine pounds, and the king size only five pounds. The giant box weighs two pounds.

Eggs: a jumbo egg is large, extra large is regular, large is a small egg and medium you need two.

This all comes to mind now because it's Christmas and some of us are trying to buy clothes for our friends as presents. Clothes sizes are the worst mess of all. I wear a size 8½ shoe but I wear a size 11 sock. Does this make any sense? On the same foot?

Why does every piece of clothing have a different size scale? Why do I wear a size 7½ hat but a size 16½ shirt collar?

Doesn't that sound as though I could put my shirt on over my hat with my collar buttoned? Why is the average suit size for a man a 40 and the average dress size for a woman a 12? We're not *that* much bigger.

Every year I go into a store wanting to buy a present for one of my daughters. I know what she looks like but I don't see her every day anymore. The clerk says, "How big is she?"

I say, "Well, you know, about—well, you know, not very big."

"Is she my size?"

"Yeah, she's about your size, but not quite so—you know."

Well, the clerk doesn't know at all, of course, and I have very little chance of getting anything that fits. The average woman might wear a size 12 dress, 34 blouse, size 6 shoe, size 10 stocking and a size 7 glove. If you go to a real fancy store and want to buy something made in France, of course, that's different. A size 12 is about a 42, unless she's a junior.

Merry Christmas. You can always take it back.

MAIL

Why is it we all look forward to the mail coming every day?

It's as if we were always getting money or good news from someone. That's not what I get. I doubt if one out of every ten pieces of mail that comes to my house is anything I want. You know, what you'd call a real letter.

This comes to mind now because I just got the darnedest box of mail you ever saw. Some woman in New Jersey—her name is Alice—saved up all the mail she got last year asking for money and sent it to me.

How can I ever thank you enough, Alice? Alice didn't even open most of it. I've never met her, but you can tell a lot about her from the mail she's gotten: the Salvation Army, Boy Scouts of America, UNICEF, National Indian Youth Council. Alice is in favor of protecting the environment, too. You can tell that. She likes animals. All good groups, but why do they gang up on this poor woman? She told me in a letter that she gave to just one of these environmental groups and that one passed her name along to all the others.

Some of them realize you're going to throw their letter away without reading it, so they try to get your attention on the envelope: *"Please return the enclosed questionnaire within 10 days."* Under threat of death, presumably!

"LAST CHANCE!" one says. If there's one thing you can be sure of, it's that when an envelope comes saying last chance on it, they'll give you another chance later.

Here's one trick: if you want to know who gives your name away or sells it to someone else, the thing to do is to give yourself a fake middle initial when you send money to any organization; then every time a letter comes addressed that way, you'll know where it came from.

The thing that bothers me most, I suppose, is that if you give twenty-five dollars to a school or a college or some good cause, they'll turn around and spend fifty dollars trying to get you to give more. I see that Alice has given to the United Negro College Fund. I gave twenty-five dollars to the NAACP years ago, and I'll bet the NAACP and the United Negro College Fund have spent a hundred dollars in stamps trying to get more from me since then.

The postal service says that they handle 97 billion pieces of mail a year but that only 20 percent of that is mail from one citizen to another. The commercial mail business says it would cost us all a lot more if it wasn't for them.

I think I'm willing to pay.

LETTERS

Every night when I get home, there's a little pile of mail waiting for me. I used to think I'd find something wonderful in the pile, but I never do.

I got thinking about the kind of letters I wish I'd receive and never do. I had to write these myself.

Dear Classmate:

Just a note to tell you there won't be any annual fund-raising drive this year. Because of the warm winter, the University's fuel bill was less than expected and, by firing some of the dead wood on the faculty, they've been able to stay way under budget and won't need any money.

Sincerely,

Ham Davis, Class Secretary

Mr. Andy Rooney
60 MINUTES
524

SAN DIEGO
PM
24 MAR
1981

Street
501

FRANCIS
PARKMAN

15¢

US Postage
B

SANTA ANA CA 92711
MAR
1981

Mr. Andy Rooney
"60 Minutes"
524 W. 57th St.   10019
New York, N.Y.

r. Andy Roone
o 60 Minute
4 West 57th
w York, New

Randy Collins
1587 Charles Ct.
Arcata, Ca. 95521

March 29th

Mr. Andy Rooney
c/o 60 Minutes
524 W. 57th St.
N.Y.   10019

Here's one from a restaurant I ate in the other night.

Dear Mr. Rooney:
   In checking your bill, we noticed that the total was $57.30 for four people, not the $63.40 we charged you. Our check for $6.10 is enclosed.

This is one I never got from the New York City Police Department.

Dear Sir or Madame:
   Please ignore the parking ticket which was placed on the windshield of your vehicle in error. We regret any inconvenience this may have caused you.

Here's one I'd like to get from an insurance company.

Dear Rooney:
   You can drop dead as far as the Pilgrim Fathers Life Insurance Company is concerned. We've tried to sell you a policy for the past twenty years. You've never answered one request for information about yourself yet. This is the last letter you'll ever get from us, fella!

Well, I sincerely hope so, Pilgrim Fathers.
And here's a letter I'd like to get from a contractor working on my house

Dear Mr. Rooney:
   Enclosed is the bill for the addition to your home. Our estimate for the job was $6,700, but because of problems we thought we'd have that we didn't run into, we were able to complete it for only $5,100.

                              Martin Construction Company

41

And after a year of getting letters like those, here's a little note I'd like to find in my mailbox just before Christmas, with a ten-dollar bill attached to it.

> Dear Mr. Rooney:
>
> It's been such a pleasure serving you this year that I want you to accept this little token of my appreciation.
>
> Signed,
Your mailman

Nice?

MOST NEEDED

What I've done here is make a list of The Most Needed Things in America.

—To start with, we need a telephone that lets you know who's calling before you answer it. I always think it's going to be someone wonderful and it almost never is.

—We need a car that gets fifty miles to a gallon, won't rust out after two winters with salt on the roads and can't go faster than the speed limit. I approve of the 55-mile limit but I often drive faster than that. I shouldn't . . . and I wouldn't if I couldn't.

—America needs a new kind of politician. We need a Presidential candidate who is smart enough not to want such a terrible job.

—We need an umbrella that doesn't have a handle up the middle, right where you want to stand when it's raining.

—We need a prison in which to put our worst criminals. It

should be secure enough so they'd never get out, but comfortable enough for them so the rest of us wouldn't feel terrible about keeping them in it for the rest of their lives. It should be a self-supporting community.

—I hate to suggest another public agency, but we need one whose only job would be to keep a brief record of each of our lives. When any one of us dies, that record will be filed away permanently. Anyone living in the distant future will be able to look us up and find out a little about us. We've lost too many people.

—I call on Congress to pass two laws. The first would decree that henceforth there would be no overlapping of professional sports. Baseball, being a spring-and-summer sport, would have to end before football, a fall sport, began.

—The second law would concern Congress itself. In the future, we'd be able to write to Congressmen free of charge. It would cost *them* money to write to us.

—The next item concerns television. We need a television set that turns off automatically when a show gets bad enough. If they can make fire alarms that smell smoke, I don't see why a device can't be made that would detect a bad television show.

—The last thing we need is some new national emergencies. I think we're all sick and tired of oil and inflation.

Those are some of the things we need in America.

RATINGS

I rate things one to ten.

One to ten ought to be our standard for rating everything. We need just one system and that's the best one.

Most schools grade students' work as A, B, C, D or F . . . five grades. Teachers aren't satisfied with five, so they start giving C pluses and D minuses. With a plus and a minus for five grades, that gives you fifteen. It's too many. Fifteen is for people who can't make up their minds how to rate something.

Perhaps you ask, "What are some of the things *you* rate from one to ten?" Well, I'll tell you some.

- *Charlie's Angels,* I give a three.
- Wonder Bread, one.
- Zbigniew Brzezinski, six.
- Scotch Tape, seven.
- Nixon's book, three.

- Howard Johnson's peppermint ice cream, nine.
- Golden retrievers, ten.
- Kleenex, eight.
- Schenectady, New York, five.
- General Eisenhower, ten.
- President Eisenhower, four.
- Vladimir Horowitz, ten.
- Rochelle Hudson, four.
- MacNeil/Lehrer, nine.
- Two-dollar bills, three.
- Howard Cosell, one.

It's fun to do. You can sit around nights and make a game of it, making a list of things and rating them . . . *Time* magazine . . . Disneyland . . . the post office . . . California . . . airline food . . . *Star Wars*. I mean, the list is endless.

If we all used the one-to-ten system of grading everything in our lives, it would make decisions quicker and easier.

Prejudice has gotten a bad name recently but prejudice is a great help to us in our lives. If we know what we think and where we rate things, we don't have to waste a lot of time thinking them through again. I rate liver one. I *know* I dislike liver and I don't ever want to try another piece.

The way to end a cute piece like this would be for me to give it a rating from one to ten. I rate television people who put endings like that on pieces like this, two.

and I thought this was just an after-theater snack." And we said, "Thank you, maybe another day." And the lady winked at me and she said, "Well, we'll try again."

ROONEY (to camera):

The surprising thing about the Palace is how good it is. The food is excellent. As a matter of fact, I plan to come over here real often . . . and bring the kids.

Two of the best lunches I ever had, I ate standing up . . . and within an hour of each other. Both places serve the same thing, oysters. Felix's is on Iberville Street in New Orleans and the Acme Oyster House is right across from it.

Every restaurant has its own way of doing things and if you don't know what it is, it's easy to look dumb the first time you go in a place.

ROONEY:

What is the difference between the ones that are three dollars a dozen and the ones that are two-seventy-five?

MAN (cutting oysters open):

. . . table.

ROONEY:

Oh, the table. If I eat them at the table, they're more? Are some of them harder to open than others?

MAN:

Some of them are hard, some of them's easy.

ROONEY:

But they're alive until you open them, is that right?

MAN:

Yes, sir.

ROONEY:

You mean I just ate a dozen live oysters?

It's always hard to find a good place to eat when you're driving in an unfamiliar part of the country, particularly if there are three or four people in the car who don't agree where you're going to eat. You get to one place and it looks fair but you decide to pass it up. You drive ten miles and you wish you'd stopped there, usually.

The trouble with most country inns is the same thing that's wrong with so many restaurants. They're fake, an imitation of the real thing.

The food in most country inns now comes from the city . . . frozen.

Being good at picking a place to eat is a matter of experience . . . prejudice acquired over years of eating out.

Deciding which restaurant *not* to go to is important. . . .There are little things you look for.

I have as many as fifty little reasons for steering clear of certain places. Just for example:

- I am very suspicious of a restaurant that says it is Polynesian and has flaming torches outside.
- If a Chinese restaurant serves chop suey and chow mein, I assume that it isn't very good . . . or very Chinese.
- Cute names on restaurants, such as Dew Drop Inn, suggest that the owners aren't very serious about their food. Watch out for places named after a new movie.
- Places that advertise "Home Cooking" don't interest me. If I want home cooking, I'll eat home.
- And I'm put off if there's a sign in the window saying "OPEN." Restaurants with OPEN signs usually leave them there even when they're closed.
- I'm not attracted to an establishment that puts more emphasis on liquor than on food.
- Usually I avoid a restaurant located in a shopping center.
- And if a restaurant is connnected with a bowling alley, it isn't where I'm going to spend my money for food.
- I don't eat where there's music either. Sometimes two things that are great by themselves are ruined when mixed. Food and entertainment are best kept apart.
- It's hard enough to get waited on in a restaurant that thinks it has enough help without going to one with a sign in the window advertising for waiters.
- And when I stay in a hotel or a motel, I never eat in the restaurant attached to it unless it's snowing.

There are just as many things that attract me to a restaurant:

- I'm a sucker for a place bearing the first name of the owner. If it's called "Joe's," I go in.

- I'm attracted to a restaurant that has a menu written with chalk on a slate.
- And to me, a real sign of class is a restaurant that refuses to accept credit cards.

If you've always thought of a menu as just a list of food a restaurant serves, you're wrong. Menus are a big business by themselves and a lot of restaurants spend a fortune making theirs look good.

We went down to a studio one day when they were filming a new cover for a Howard Johnson menu. The food was fixed in a kitchen near the studio. They try to be honest about it . . . but nothing ever looks *smaller* in the picture on the menu. For instance, they weigh the meat all right, but then they barely cook it so it doesn't shrink.

In the course of doing this report, we've looked through and collected several hundred menus. You can tell a lot about a restaurant from a quick look at its menu . . . even from the outside of it. For instance, if there's a tassel on the menu, you can add a couple of dollars per person.

Here's the Captain's Seafood Platter. The trouble with a restaurant called the Captain's Seafood Platter in Kansas City is that all the fish comes frozen, and by the time it's cooked in hot fat, you can't tell the oysters from the French fries.

The Lion's Paw . . . "Homemade Cheesecake." You always wonder whose home they mean it was made in.

Don Neal's Mr. T-Bone. He's a musician, I guess. This is the kind of a menu that's so cute you can hardly tell what they have to eat. "Rhapsody of Beef" . . . Roast Top Sirloin. "Symphony of the Deep" . . . Baked Lake Superior Whitefish. "Taste Buds in Concert" . . . Breast of Chicken Almondine.

Here's a place called the Bali Hai, a Polynesian restaurant. The "Pu-Pu Platter," they have. "Shrimp Pago Pago." I never know about the drinks in a place like this. Here's one called "Scorpion Bowl." I hate drinking from a glass with a naked girl on it.

This is a Spanish restaurant, La Corrida. Picture of a bullfight. They've just killed the bull, I guess.

I'm not a vegetarian, but I hate being reminded of the animals I'm eating. I'll eat almost anything, too, but there are a few things I'm narrow-minded about. Rabbit I don't eat, tripe, calves' brains, snails. I know I'm wrong, but I just don't eat them.

Karson's Inn in Historic Canton. This is one of those menus that tell you more about a town than you want to know. "Welcome to Karson's Inn in Historic Canton. . . ." It goes on and tells you all about how interesting Canton is.

Here's one from Troggio's in New Castle, Pennsylvania. This one tells you about how interesting New Castle is.

This is the Lamplighter, a family restaurant. It's one of those where they tell you about the family. "For over 50 years the Ferri Family has enjoyed serving the finest food to nice people like you. . . ." They like me.

This is another one: the Presuttis'. Mama and Poppa Presutti are on the cover there. And, yep, they tell you about the Presuttis here. "In 1933, Mr. and Mrs. S. Presutti converted their home into a restaurant." It goes on. You know, fine, but what have they got to eat?

This is something called the Shalako. It's one of those menus with a lot of writing on it. I always figure if I wanted to read, I'd go to a library. It says "The Shalako is the most important religious ceremony performed by the Zuñi Indians." And it goes on for three pages. You can imagine a waiter standing there while you read this history of the Zuñi Indians.

Here's a place called the Parlour. I wonder where this is? Oh, there is no doubt where this is: "It is dusk in St. Paul. Sunset's fading light reflects a red ribbon on the meandering

71

Mississippi River. The skyline is silhouetted against the blue-gray haze.''

A menu.

We had a not particularly reliable survey made of menus and we have the results for you. According to the count we made, the most used words on menus were these, in order of frequency.

1. ''Freshly''
2. ''Tender''
3. ''Mouth-Watering''
4. ''Succulent''
5. ''On a Bed of''
6. ''Tangy''
7. ''Hearty''

8. "Luscious"
9. "To Your Liking"
10. "Topped with"
11. "Savory"
12. "Tempting" and "Delicious" (Tie)
13. "Surrounded by"
14. "Golden Brown"
15. "By Our Chef"
16. "Seasoned to Perfection"
17. "Choice Morsels of"
18. "Delicately" and "Thick" (Tie)
19. "Crisp"
20. "Not Responsible for Personal Property"

"Freshly" was far and away the first.

"Savory," Number 11, was interesting. Actually, on menus where the dinner was more than $7.50, it was usually spelled with a "U." S-A-V-O-U-R-Y.

"Surrounded by." "Surrounded by" and "On a Bed of" are a lot the same, but "On a Bed of" actually beat out "Surrounded by."

"Golden Brown." Almost everything is "Golden Brown." Sometimes the lettuce is golden brown.

"By Our Chef." Even places that don't have a chef say "By Our Chef."

"Seasoned to Perfection." "Choice Morsels of." "Delicately" and "Thick" were tied for 18. Number 19 was "Crisp." And Number 20 on our list of most used words was "Not Responsible for Personal Property."

Wine menus. Last year was a very good year for wine menus.

Anyone who orders wine in a restaurant always wonders

how much the same bottle would cost him in a liquor store. We thought we'd find out.

ROONEY (in liquor store):
    What's the price of the Chauvenet Red Cap?
LIQUOR-STORE OWNER:
    Six-ninety-nine.
ROONEY (from menu):
    Chauvenet Red Cap . . . twenty dollars a bottle. This is at the restaurant called the Michelangelo. Let's see. Liebfraumilch, Blue Nun . . . ten dollars. (To liquor-store owner) What do you get for Blue Nun?
OWNER:
    Three-eighty-nine.
ROONEY (from menu):
    Mouton Cadet Rothschild, 1970 . . . twelve dollars. (To liquor-store owner) This Mouton Cadet. What do you get for that?
OWNER:
    Three-ninety-nine.
ROONEY:
    You don't lose any money on that, either.
OWNER:
    No.
ROONEY (from menu):
    Château Malijay . . . six-forty-five.
STORE OWNER:
    That's a Côte du Rhône . . . one-ninety-nine.
ROONEY (From menu):
    Here's a bottle of Pouilly-Fumé de la Doucette, 1971 . . . eighteen dollars. (To store owner) What do you get for that?
OWNER:
    La Doucette, Pouilly-Fumé . . . We sell it for six-ninety-nine.

ROONEY: (from menu):
This is a restaurant in Las Vegas. Here the Lancers Rosé is eleven dollars. (To store owner) Lancers Vin Rosé?

OWNER:
Lancers sells for four-twenty-nine.

ROONEY:
I always thought this was the kind of a wine where the bottle was worth more than the drink. I guess you wouldn't want to comment on that?

OWNER:
No, I'd rather not.

Everyone complains about wine snobs. Snobs of every kind have a bad reputation in America. No one understands that it's the snobs who set the standards of excellence in the world. There are art snobs, literary snobs, music snobs, and in every case it's the snobs who sneer at mediocrity. The gourmets are the food snobs. Without them we'd all be eating peanut-butter sandwiches.

Like the gourmets, wine snobs know what they're talking about. So if you're going to drink wine, get to know something about it. Be prepared to pay too much for a bottle of wine. Be your own wine snob . . . it's part of the fun.

A good rule of thumb is, if you can afford a wine, don't buy it.

I went to the National Restaurant Association Convention in Chicago and everywhere I wandered someone was pushing food or drink at me.

Everyone who sells anything to restaurants had an exhibit, so there were garbage cans . . . corn cookers . . . can openers . . .

wall decorations . . . seating arrangements . . . and devices to keep bartenders from stealing.

Restaurants sell 20 percent of all the food eaten in the United States. They are first in the number of retail business places. In other words, there are more restaurants than any other kind of store. We did a lot of poking around at the convention and we got a frightening look at what some restaurants are going to be feeding us.

1ST EXHIBITOR:
    Well, this is a soy protein with about 60 percent protein and it goes into . . .
ROONEY:
    What does it do?
1ST EXHIBITOR:
    Well, it stretches out products like tuna salad by about 30 percent.
ROONEY:
    What do they use it in, in addition to tuna fish?
1ST EXHIBITOR:
    It goes into egg salads. It's used to extend all kinds of meats, either uncooked as meat patties or it might go into precooked entrees . . . sloppy Joes, chili con carne.
ROONEY:
    Is it any good?
1ST EXHIBITOR:
    What kind of a question is that?
ROONEY:
    Now, what is this here?
2ND EXHIBITOR:
    These are our Morning Star institutional link-sausage-like flavor product.
ROONEY:
    Sausage . . . like?

2ND EXHIBITOR:
Sausage-like flavor.

ROONEY:
They're artificial sausage?

2ND EXHIBITOR:
They're artificial sausage. They have no cholesterol, no animal fat.

ROONEY:
What *do* they have?

2ND EXHIBITOR:
Well, they're made out of various vegetable proteins . . . soy protein, wheat protein. We use egg albumen to hold it together.

ROONEY:

Are you a chef?

2ND EXHIBITOR:

No. I'm trained as a biochemist.

ROONEY:

Now what is this machine?

3RD EXHIBITOR:

This is a mechanical meat tenderizer.

ROONEY:

You put the meat on there?

3RD EXHIBITOR:

Put the meat on here. It'll pass through underneath the needle. The needle will come down and penetrate the meat and break down the tissue.

ROONEY:

So a restaurant could buy this and really buy less expensive meat?

3RD EXHIBITOR:

That's right.

ROONEY:

Now, I would call that orange juice canned. Not fresh.

4TH EXHIBITOR:

Fresh frozen.

ROONEY:

Fresh frozen. Right.

ROONEY (looking at ingredients):

Now, "standard chicken base." How do you pronounce that ingredient?

5TH EXHIBITOR:

It contains hydrolyzed vegetable protein.

ROONEY (reads ingredients):

"Salt, chicken fat, monosodium glutamate, dehydrated chicken, dextrose, dehydrated vegetable, spices and spice extract, bicalcium phosphate, citric acid."

5TH EXHIBITOR:

Right.

ROONEY:

That's chicken base?

5TH EXHIBITOR:

That's right.

ROONEY:

It tastes like chicken?

5TH EXHIBITOR:

Exactly. Four ounces of it tastes like an extra gallon.

ROONEY:

You put just four ounces of this hydro . . .

5TH EXHIBITOR:

And that's the basis for, in other words, if you want chicken noodle, you throw noodles in.

ROONEY:

How many restaurants *don't* use anything like this?

5TH EXHIBITOR:

Almost 100 percent of the restaurants use it. If they don't, then you're way on the other side of the . . . You can't exist today.

ROONEY:

You mean without the artificial stuff?

5TH EXHIBITOR:

It's not artificial really. You've got monosodium glutamate. You've got extracts. You've got fats. The real thing mixed with the chemical. This can feed or this can substitute or feed a thousand people per chicken, where you might have to take a hundred chickens. . . .

ROONEY:

The chickens must love it.

5TH EXHIBITOR:

You're a nice fellow.

* * *

Restaurants are one of the few good examples left of really free enterprise in America. There isn't much government control of them and the good ones prosper. The bad ones usually, though not always, go out of business.

The best restaurants are operated by people who like food better than money. The worst ones are run by people who don't know anything about food *or* money.

So that's our report on eating out in America. The camera crew is glad it's over because they say they're tired of spending their dinner hour watching me eat.

During the time we've been working on it, many friends and others here at CBS have been stopping me in the hallway to ask one question. It's a question I haven't mentioned so far in the broadcast. . . .

But the answer, as of this morning . . . fourteen pounds.

Surroundings

ON THE HOUSE

One of the most popular topics of conversation for homeowners is how much more their houses are worth now than when they bought them. It's a very dull topic and it's silly because we all know that if you sell a house for twice what you paid, you buy another for twice what someone else paid for that one. If you don't sell your house, it doesn't make any difference how much it's worth to anyone but you anyway, and not selling your house always seemed to make more sense to me.

There are 218 million people in the United States and 40 million houses for them to buy. There are as many different kinds of houses as there are different kinds of people: new houses, old houses, wooden houses, stone houses, brick houses, wonderfully substantial-looking houses, and houses that blow away in the wind, houses all together in a row and houses all by themselves out in the middle of miles and miles of no-other-houses.

Most towns have one funny-looking house. Everyone laughs at it, but the people who live in it like it. Then there's the big house, owned by the rich grouch or by the widow of the man who owned the mill; the stately and beautiful home that everyone dreams of living in; the house that's just a little too obviously the product of a young architect's imagination.

Houses come in a variety of shapes, too. There are square houses, round houses, six-sided houses. There are even some eight-sided houses. A geodesic house is all sides and an igloo has none. Some houses are tall, some are short. There are houses that look like mushrooms and houses built like arches.

There are permanent little villages of comfortable homes nestled in the valleys across the country and contagious outbreaks of immobile mobile homes that pock the face of the landscape. If they're mobile, why don't they go?

People seem less sentimental about where they live these days. Maybe it's because not as many houses are homes or because they have no family in the cemetery in town. Maybe people are less sentimental about where they live now because they don't spend much time there. The new houses are efficient workshops, set up so that what has to be done can be done quickly, though without joy, so the people who own them can leave for someplace else. The getaway car is always ready in the driveway.

It used to be that home was a place to stay in and enjoy. The house had been built by a carpenter who did it from a plan in his head. There are rooms in those houses that weren't

85

designed for anything special. There were usually four or five bedrooms, a living room, a parlor, a big kitchen, but then there were spare rooms. The builder didn't have any idea what you were going to do with your spare room. It wasn't his business. You could make up what the room was for as you went along living. There was always one floor above the top floor, too, the attic.

An attic was maybe the best place ever invented for a house and it's too bad they're a thing of the past. The family treasures from generations back were stored up there. Halloween costumes weren't bought; they were made up from something dug out of a trunk in the attic.

Many of the old houses are deteriorating now, of course. They're too big to heat, too much to take care of. An old house takes a lot of love. A modern house doesn't take much love but it doesn't give much either.

Every town or city should have some rich people, but the big estates with expansive lawns are being chopped into tiny pieces for middle-income housing projects. No one has time to mow an acre of lawn and not many of us have the money to get it mowed for us. The people who have the money can't find anyone who wants to do it. Now a little patch of green will do. Mowing the lawn isn't much more than an extension of vacuuming the living room.

In hundreds of places, the biggest, grandest, most interesting house in town has been repaired, repainted, landscaped and restored to its original beauty . . . to be used as a funeral home.

Modern houses aren't so much built as they are produced. The houses are put up not one at a time but in clusters, each house having all the individuality of a slice of Wonder bread. It would be wrong to say there aren't some beautiful and livable modern houses. Of course there are, just as there are miserable old houses. The trouble with so many modern

houses is that someone else has decided where things are going to go. Everything is built in, recessed and right at your fingertips, even if that isn't where you want it.

The trouble with a house like that is finding a place to put the debris of your life that you love. Where do kids hide on each other in houses like that?

The next best thing to an attic they've stopped putting on houses is a porch. If they put anything out front now, it's a little cement square which has none of the grace of a porch even if you stick two plastic chairs on it.

People seem more backyard than front porch oriented now. They're turning their backs on a world they used to face. They're looking for privacy, hiding behind fences. What used to go on the front porch is taking place out back now behind the fence around the patio.

People seem to miss their front porches too. You see them inventing makeshift substitutes. There's something satisfying about sitting out in front of your very own house, watching the world go by. It's your house and there you are, out in front of it. You're available to be seen and can, in turn, watch the passing parade or just sit there, reading the paper, if there's no parade.

A porch made a perfect first step away from home for a child too young to cross the street. Wheeled toys rolled there in the rain, and on hot summer evenings young lovers rocked in their own breeze.

As the porch disappeared, we entered into a new era of garage-door dominance. This ranks as one of the major architectural and aesthetic disasters of all time. What you see when you look at a house like that is garage doors. The small area to one side of the garage doors is the house.

Almost all of the 40 million single-family houses in this country have garages, many of them built for two cars. The

ultimate status symbol is a three-car garage. A three-car garage announces affluence.

It's a funny thing, though, no matter how many garages there are in America, it is very unlikely that more than a million of the 90 million cars we have ever gets put in one. For one thing, they don't fit. Almost no one can put even one of their cars in their two-car garage. The cars have been driven out by the lawnmowers, the bicycles and most important, of course, the indispensable junk. Sometimes people can't even get their car into the driveway leading to the garage. The worst thing, of course, is when you can't even get all the junk in the garage. Some people have even found the garage too valuable a space to be wasted on a car, so they convert it into a room.

A lot of people who are wonderfully good grounds-keepers

landscape the exterior of their home and then ruin the effect by parking a battered hulk of a car or truck out front. As a matter of fact, you can usually tell almost everything about the people inside a house by looking at the outside of the house. There are people you know must live well-ordered lives. Their lawns are mowed and you know their checkbooks are, no doubt, balanced.

And then there are the more expansive types. They bite off more than they can chew with a house. They fill their lives and their backyards with just a little more than a life or a backyard can hold and their backyards runneth over.

The average American moves once every five years or thirteen times in his lifetime. That means that 20 percent of the population moves every year. They pick up their worldly possessions and take off. Everyone is going somewhere else.

I don't know why people are moving so often these days. No house is perfect but you learn to live with it after you've been in one a few years. Like your own shortcomings, you find ways to ignore the imperfections of a house when it's your home.

There are reverberations of the past everywhere in a house you've lived in for a long time. It isn't a sad place, though, because all the things left undone hold great hope for future Saturday mornings. The house you live in isn't a potential real-estate listing in tomorrow's paper. It isn't a Holiday Inn or a temporary shelter to keep you warm and dry for the night before the hunt begins tomorrow. Your house is your home, an anchor, a place to go when you don't want to go anyplace.

STREET NAMES

What would you think, just offhand, is the most common street name in the United States? Pretend you win a hundred dollars if you guess right.

You'd have to say that, overall, we haven't shown a lot of originality with the names we've given our streets. In most countries the great streets have great names. London has half a dozen of them: Bond Street, Fleet Street, Carnaby Street, Piccadilly; Paris has the Champs-Elysées; Berlin the Unter den Linden; Leningrad the Nevsky Prospekt.

What do we have? Michigan Boulevard. Sunset Boulevard. Some of our great streets don't even have names; they have numbers. In New York the classiest street in town is called Fifth Avenue; some of the numbers in New York are even dull. Forty-second Street. Would you write a song about a street with a name like that?

So, have you given any thought to the most common street

name? Main? Wrong. Not even close. I'll give them to you in reverse order, like a Miss America contest. The fifth most common street name in America according to postal service records is (*music: sting*) Lincoln!

The fourth most common name is . . . Oak. Third, Maple. The second most common is Washington. And the winner, the single most frequently used name for a street in all the U.S. is . . . Park! Park Street, Park Avenue, Park Terrace, Park Something is the winner.

Of the twenty-five most common street names, seven are former Presidents, nine are trees. Franklin is the only person's name in the first twenty-five who wasn't a President. If you thought Broadway or Main were in there, you were really wrong. Main is thirty-second and Broadway isn't even in the first fifty.

Street names don't usually make much sense when you get thinking about them. If a street is named Wolf Lane, it's usually been a hundred years since anyone saw a wolf around there. Very often there's no view of the bay from Bay View, no oak trees left on Oak Street and no hill anywhere around most of Hillside.

These days there's nothing interesting about the way a street gets its name. What happens most often is that a developer comes along and builds a bunch of houses all in a row (and they're all made of ticky-tack). At some point he realizes that if he's going to advertise them for sale they have to have an address, so he thinks up a cute name for the street and for the rest of its life that's what it's called.

The names of streets in developments lack the same character the development lacks and are at least fitting in this respect. Developers very often try to lend class to an area by calling it something other than a street. They call it a lane, a terrace or a circle. They'll call it Dogwood Lane on the theory that you can ask more for a house on a lane than one on a street. A really exclusive street has bumps build into the road so no one can drive very fast. Built-in bumps are restricted to the classiest, most expensive development streets.

There is one mystery that remains unsolved in regard to street names in America. According to our count, Third Street was the seventeenth most popular street name. I accept that, but Second Street was nineteenth most common and what about First Street? First Street was thirtieth!

Now what in the world ever happened to all the First Streets in cities that have Second and Third Streets? And how come there are more Thirds than Seconds?

BANK NAMES

Thousands of you have written asking me to explain how they name a bank. How, you ask, do they come up with a name when they sit down and decide to start up a place for us to keep our money—or more accurately, a place for *them* to keep our money.

Well, it isn't like naming a child or a dog or even another business. A bank has to have a name that sounds important and honest, otherwise people would keep their money under the mattress where it belongs.

If a bank has connections in Washington, there's a law that says it has to call itself either National or Federal. After that, they can do what they want with their name and very few of them are satisfied with just one name like that, so they embellish it with something they feel makes it sound better.

They'll call themselves United National, Century National, Sterling National or Cosmopolitan National. National Bank of Pike City, National Bank of America, National Bank of Utah are all bank names. In Washington there's even a Hemisphere National Bank.

Just as banks are not satisfied being just plain National, neither are they happy being simply Federal. They prefer being Columbia Federal, Independence Federal, Metropolitan Federal or, perhaps, Central or Midwest Federal.

They may also be County or State Federal. This would seem to be a contradiction to many of us but not to the people who name banks. They don't seem to worry much about making sense with their names. It's just got to have the right ring to it. Perpetual Federal Savings is the actual name of a bank.

The greatest bank name in America and perhaps in the world is the National Home Permanent Federal Savings and Loan. That has just about everything anyone would possibly want in a bank name. They don't make it clear whether it's the savings or the loan that's permanent but that's one of the mysteries that keeps us all interested in banks.

If there is one tiny element missing in that name, it is the ever-popular bank word "American." Banks like being American-this, American-that. And then there are the banks that prefer simplicity to patriotism. Home Savings is a simple name. Or Farm and Home Savings. Would a bank named Farm and Home Savings cheat you?

Some banks get stuck with a name that sounded good a hundred years ago when they were founded but sounds sort of silly now. In New York there's a Dime Savings Bank. Once you pass forty, a dime isn't worth bending over to pick up if you drop one. You certainly wouldn't bother to take it to a bank to save it.

"Trust" is a word banks like in their names although it's a two-faced word. Banks use it in its financial sense and the rest of us think of it as meaning dependable. Banks like to have us think that about them and they are also suggesting they trust *us*—which we know isn't true.

Irving Trust . . . the National Savings and Trust . . . Bankers

Trust. Bankers Trust is a big organization with a lot of customers, but who bankers trust is mostly each other.

Banks not only like being National, Federal, American, Home and Trusted, they also like being First. The First National Bank of Almost Anywhere, First Union Bank, First Savings and Loan. (In New York there's a Ninth Federal. This is strange because where there's a First Federal, there doesn't seem to be any Second, Third or Fourth Federal, let alone an Eighth. Bookkeeping error, probably.)

One of the newest banks is called the First Women's Bank. I suppose it won't be long before we get a Gay Trust.

Just as there are names banks favor, there are names they'd never think of using. Certain businesses seem to preempt groups of names for themselves. Acme, for instance, is most apt to be an exterminating service or a dry cleaner. You wouldn't call a bank the Acme Permanent Home Trust. AAA is a name reserved for car-repair shops and people who fix radiators.

Bel Air is popular everywhere as the name of a roadside motel. You wouldn't find a Bel Air Bank in any town that wasn't called Bel Air itself. Nor would any financial institution call itself a Bankorama or Bankland or Bank City. Those are supermarket names.

Banks often spend a lot of money having a trademark designed for them too. They'll have something like a rolling wheel within an octagon that has all sorts of symbolic meaning to someone. The New York Bank for Savings uses a beehive as its symbol. This seems odd because we all know what happens to the bee. He works his tail off all summer saving honey for the tough times ahead and then some smart guy with a net over his head comes along and takes it all away from him.

And that's how banks are named.

FENCES

Our brains have a way of jumping around a lot, thinking of one thing for a few seconds and then flitting off to think of another. For me as a writer, it's always been fun to see if I could stop one subject in my head for long enough to take a good look at it.

For instance, I was thinking about fences. There are as many kinds of fences in this country as there are people. You couldn't *count* all the kinds of fences there are. There are big fences, small fences, teeny-tiny fences.

The biggest difference between one fence and another fence is whether the fence was built to protect what's inside from what's outside or to protect what's outside from what's inside. To protect the people outside, for instance, a mean dog has to be fenced in.

It's a mystery why some fences are ever built at all. Most cemeteries have fences, even though no one outside really wants to get in and no one inside ever tries to get out.

Sometimes you can't tell what a fence is keeping in—or keeping out. You can't tell what a fence is protecting from what. You suspect that sometimes people just put up fences from habit, or as a show of strength or wealth. I hate anyone who has a fence that cost more than my house cost.

The best-looking fences are often the simplest. A simple fence around a beautiful home can be like a frame around a picture. The house isn't hidden; its beauty is enhanced by the frame. But a fence can be a massive, ugly thing, too, made of bricks and mortar. Sometimes the insignificant little fences do their job just as well as the ten-foot walls. Maybe it's only a string stretched between here and there in a field. The message is clear: don't cross here.

There's often a question about whether a barrier is a fence

or a wall. Fences, I think, are thinner than walls. And, of course, there are people who confuse us further by building fences on *top* of walls.

Every fence has its own personality and some don't have much. There are friendly fences. A friendly fence takes kindly to being leaned on. There are friendly fences around playgrounds. And some playground fences are more fun to play on than anything they surround. There are more mean fences than friendly fences overall, though. Some have their own built-in invitation not to be sat upon. Unfriendly fences get it right back sometimes. You seldom see one that hasn't been hit, bashed, bumped or in some way broken or knocked down.

One of the phenomena of fences is their tendency to proliferate. Note, if you will, how often one fence brings on another fence. People often seem to want their own fence, even if it's back to back, cheek by jowl with the neighbor's fence, almost as though the fence was put up to keep the fence out.

The other thing I thought about fences: I thought maybe the world wouldn't be very much changed if tomorrow morning . . . every fence was gone.

PUBLIC ART

If you're putting up pictures in your own house, you can decide for yourself what looks good and how much you want to pay to have it look that way. Decorating a city with works of art is a lot harder.

Nothing in this country has changed more than our public art, and a lot of people don't like it. For a long while, the statues in little parks everywhere were in the image of traditional old American heroes, or perhaps some local hero known only to the people of the town where it stood. There were tens of thousands of Civil War statues put up, and tens of thousands more memorializing the doughboys of World War I.

Statues erected in honor of people who were heroic after 1930 are rare. Maybe heroes are rarer. Sculptors have always liked to make horses. Anyone looks heroic on a horse.

There was never much complaining about the money spent

on heroic statuary. I suppose people aren't so apt to complain about art in honor of the dead.

That's not true about the new, modern sculptures being put up everywhere with both public and private money. It seems to many people that artists are trying too hard to be artistic. Most people like art to look like things as they know them to be. That's hard for an artist, and skeptics think that's why artists have changed what they do. If it doesn't look like anything we know, we can't complain that it doesn't look like what it's supposed to. It isn't *supposed* to look like anything.

A lot of the most modern work has been commissioned by the federal government. Most of us don't have very good taste in art, but government's taste is usually worse.

People who like the modern public art refer to it as a museum without walls.

Critics who *don't* like it call it nonsense and a waste of money.

A good artist tries to satisfy himself. That's a noble artistic idea, but when the artist is satisfying himself with public money, he has to satisfy some other people, too.

Many modern artists work in geometric shapes. They like angles, circles, cylinders. They mix them, balance them, stand them on end. Most of us aren't ready for it. We know the artist is trying to tell us something, but it's a foreign language and we don't understand what it is he's trying to say. We'd like to see the artist's idea written out on paper in English just once. A lot of us suspect the artist of not having any idea at all, beyond getting a government grant. We aren't sure enough, though, of our own artistic judgment to say so. We know from experience that the artist may be an artistic Einstein whose work is important and great and just beyond our comprehension.

The real question is this: Is America ready for art that's smarter than it is?

SIGNS

Someone's always trying to push us around with the signs they put up, aren't they? I mean, what's your reaction when you come up against this sign: "KEEP OUT"? Even if I don't want to go in, my reaction is always: "The hell with you, fella, I'm comin' in!"

I think most of us have some kind of reaction to every sign we see that isn't the one the people who put up the sign intended us to have. For instance, when I see this one: "NO PARKING AT ANY TIME. VIOLATORS WILL BE TOWED AWAY AT OWNER'S EXPENSE," I figure they're bluffing. They've had the sign up for nine years and haven't towed away anyone yet.

A lot of signs try to scare you into not doing something: "NO TRESPASSING." "WARNING: TRESPASSERS WILL BE PUNISHED." Or maybe they'll suggest you're going to get bit: "BEWARE OF DOG!"

Some signs are very polite. For instance, they'll try to

sweet-talk you into not smoking: "THANK YOU FOR NOT SMOKING." Some are more direct: "SMOKING NOT PERMITTED." Some get tougher: "POSITIVELY NO SMOKING." "NO SMOKING— BY ORDER OF THE BOARD OF EDUCATION." Has any kid ever not done anything by order of the Board of Education?

Schools have a special, irritating way with signs. They pretend to be friendly—"WELCOME TO OUR SCHOOL"—but then tell you all the stuff you can't do: "NO BIKE RIDING, LACROSSE PLAYING, LOITERING, ETC." . . . Any kid reading it never would have thought of playing lacrosse on Sunday until he saw the sign.

I don't care much for signs with pictures of things on them: "DEER CROSSING," "CATTLE CROSSING." By the time I've figured out what it's a picture of, I'm past it.

I like signs there's no doubt about. I mean, this would only have one meaning: "IN." Here's a big new bestseller for people who make signs: "NO RIGHT TURN ON RED." We passed a law saying you *could* turn right on red; now we're putting signs up everywhere saying "Except here."

I always figure "NO THRU TRAFFIC" means it's a shortcut, but they don't want you to go that way. And "NO EXIT" *is* an exit, but they don't want you to go out that way.

There are a few signs you don't fool around with, such as "RADIATION." I mean, if you really didn't want anybody walking on your grass, that might be the one to put up.

A lot of signs are put up too late, of course. Usually by the time anyone puts up "NO DUMPING ALLOWED," people have been dumping there for ten years.

You know some signs don't really mean it. "SPEED LIMIT 5." I mean, there *is* no five miles an hour.

The fact of the matter is, most of us don't like to be told anything by a sign.

HOTELS*

One of the good things to do in life is stay in a hotel. People stay in hotels for two reasons. First, they're away from home and they need a place to sleep and leave their suitcases.

The second reason people stay in hotels is that a lot of them who are *not* neurotic and don't *mind* facing life most of the time, *enjoy* not facing it for short periods once in a while. A hotel is the ideal place for not facing life. Hotels have people who face life *for* you. All they ask of you is money.

There are about 75,000 places in the United States where more than twenty people can pay to spend the night. On an average night about two million Americans are doing that.

When people traveled on horseback or by carriage, there were roadside inns. An innkeeper was compelled by law to provide food, lodging and a place for your horse, all for one

---

*Broadcast June 28, 1966.

price. It was known as the "American Plan." Now you're more apt to find the American plan in Europe. "European Plan," more common in America, means no food and no lodging for horse or carriage.

The first real hotel in America was built in Washington, D.C., in 1793. It was called the Union Public Hotel. The City Hotel was begun the same year in New York. The first real hotel in Boston was the Tremont, built in 1827. In 1823, the 500-room National Hotel was opened in Washington. It was advertised as "The Palace of the People."

By 1850, railroad track connected most Eastern cities and was beginning to stretch west from Chicago. Wherever a train stopped, a hotel was built. In the small towns, the one hotel was a walk-with-bags from the station. Train was about the only way strangers came to town. Neither the trains, if they're still running, nor the hotels, if they're still standing, have changed much.

In the middle and late 1880s the first luxury hotels went up. They were great stone palaces built to last a thousand years. The trouble is, no one wants to stay in a thousand-

year-old hotel. Most of them have outlasted their own usefulness. They are the hotels they don't build hotels *like* anymore. Plumbing killed them.

A few of them, like the Copley Plaza in Boston, are still standing. The Plaza in New York is another grand old holdout. The management of the Plaza has never felt the need to call attention to it with a sign bearing its name. Their feeling seems to be that if you don't know where the Plaza is, you probably don't belong there.

The Brown Palace went up in Denver in 1892. That's still up. Its cavernous lobby gives the appearance of being one of those British men's clubs with high-vaulted ceilings supported by marble columns.

All hotel lobbies used to be big. You could stand around and talk with friends in them, wander around looking at things or just sit in them and watch the new people check in. People who lived in the town used the hotel lobby as a meeting place.

Those people who used to sit around hotel lobbies are gone now. I guess they're up in their rooms watching television or at the airport catching a plane for home. Lobbies are just wide places by the registration desk in new hotels. There's no income from a lobby for the hotel management and they really don't want you sitting around in it anyway. They'd rather have you in the bar, drinking.

Most of the hotels you know best if you're more than fifty years old were built in the late 1920s. Name the best-known hotel in any city and the chances are it was built then. It's the one with the roof "from high atop" which those bands emanated on late-night radio broadcasts in the 1930s. It's where you took the girl for dinner if you were serious about her. It's where you arranged to meet someone if you were downtown. Those hotels lent continuity to the life of a city just by being there.

Before all of them were called Sheraton, Hilton or Statler, hotels had good names that meant something in a community. In my hometown, Albany, New York, the two hotels were called the Ten Eyck and the De Witt Clinton. You don't mistake those names for two hotels in Des Moines, Iowa. A landmark hotel was a point of orientation in a city. Things were a block from it or ten blocks and you turned left or right at it to get somewhere.

In the 1930s, during the Depression, there was no investment capital with which to build new hotels and no one had the money to stay in one if there had been. People started traveling more by car than by train, and a new institution came into being. It was first known as the "tourist cabin" or "motor court" and later as the "motel." Most invented names don't last as well as "motel" has.

Resourceful people who couldn't find work put up a few simple buildings by the side of the road, made the beds and sold the new traveler, the car driver, a night's sleep for a dollar or two.

The emphasis is on bedrooms in the hotels that have been built in the last twenty years. While there's no income from the people sitting in the lobbies and public rooms, 70 percent of every dollar taken in on a hotel bedroom is clear profit. Once the owners have it paid for, all they have to do is provide heat and someone to come in for ten minutes a day to make the bed. If the maid spends fifteen minutes, it's probably because she's watching a soap opera on your television set and wants to wait for a commercial before she moves to the next room. The emphasis on rooms gives a hotel a pigeonhole look from the outside—but they hold a lot of pigeons.

The hotel business has always gone through alternating periods of boom and bust. During the 1960s, they were in trouble and the hotels in the worst trouble were the big old ones downtown. Most of them were built on expensive real estate near the railroad station. It was still expensive in 1968, even though the railroad station was probably all but dead and the area had turned into a slum. The classy store that used to be a block's walk had closed and reopened in the new shopping area out on the edge of town.

A lot of those good old hotels were torn down between 1960 and 1970. They had old-fashioned plumbing, makeshift air conditioning and uneconomically large public rooms and hallways. They were gracious, but most people won't pay much for grace.

The people who used to come by train and stay for two

days in a city started coming by plane. They stayed one night or not at all before they flew back out to sleep in their own beds at home. If they stayed overnight, they didn't stay downtown. They stayed in the new motel out by the airport.

Motels were the biggest problem the hotel business had, and a lot of hotel owners joined the trend. While they were tearing down great old hotels everywhere, they were erecting tacky new motels everywhere else. The real estate around all the crossroads of the major highways was bought up by motel entrepreneurs. If a traveler wants to get to a downtown hotel, he has to run a neon gauntlet of signs en route beckoning him into the roadside motel.

What motels have to offer is convenience. There they are. You register, drive your car to a spot near your room and take your own suitcases in. No one was ever really happy with bellboys. The question of how much to tip and whether you'd given him too much or too little was more than most people wanted to face.

No one has clearly defined the difference between a hotel and a motel. If you carry your own bag to your room, it's almost certainly a motel, not a hotel. It's a motel if there's a Coke machine down the hall, an ice dispenser at the top of the stairs and a small, unused swimming pool in a center area. (A lot of people who never go in a pool won't stay in a place that doesn't have one.) It's a motel if you have to keep your curtains drawn all the time.

For a while, it was a hotel if it was vertical and more than ten stories high and a motel if it was horizontal and no more than two stories. That is no longer a dependable way to differentiate between them. They've lived together for so long now that hotels and motels have crossbred, and you can't always tell one from the other. The motel chains have built what look like hotels and called them "high-rise motels." The hotel people have tried to get in on the motel business by

going to the perimeter of the city and building five-story "motor inns." They have neither the convenience of the motel nor the class of a hotel.

The big issue is the car. Something like 85 percent of all people arriving at motels or hotels come by car. Even if they fly in to the city, they rent a car at the airport.

In San Francisco one of the best hotel architects, William Tabler, designed a Hilton that tried for the best of both the hotel and the motel world. It's a hotel with a road up the middle so that you can spiral up the driveway in your car until you reach your own floor. You park, get out and carry your bag to your hotel room. Americans don't like to be far from their cars and this is the next best thing to sleeping with it under your pillow.

Most of the great big old ramshackle wooden resort hotels are gone now. In their best days, they were filled with families who had packed a steamer trunk and come there to stay from July 1st to Labor Day. The father stayed for a month.

There are still a dozen of them left to remind us of what they were. The Greenbrier and the Homestead in West Virginia, the Mackinac Island Inn, the Cloisters on Sea Island, Georgia, the Lake Placid Club, and the Broadmoor in Colorado are all still hanging on. Across the bay from San Diego, the Hotel del Coronado, built in 1888, is a reminder to Californians that there was a real world there before they came.

Those grand old resort hotels were noted chiefly for their long stretches of porch lined with sturdy, wooden rocking

116

chairs. One thing you have to say for those of us alive now, we aren't as satisfied just rocking as people used to be.

Hotels are built in most cities because there's a reason for people to come there and they need a place to stay. But then there are hotel cities where the number and quality of the hotels is part of the reason people are attracted to them. New York, Chicago, Miami, San Francisco have hotels that are themselves tourist attractions.

A good hotel room is nothing like home and that's the way we prefer it. It is refreshingly free of the miscellaneous paraphernalia that clutters our living room and our lives. Hotel managers flatter us with more towels for one day than we'd use at home in a week; they have our soap wrapped individually, put clean sheets on the bed every day and generally pretend they think we're used to being waited on.

A good hotel is a pleasure.

BASEBALL

I hate baseball. I have always hated baseball. As a matter of fact, I have a hard time liking anyone who *does* like baseball.

To be honest with you, I'll tell you it may be because I was never very good at the game. I always threw a baseball like a girl. (Is that okay to say now, or does that suggest girls don't throw baseballs very well?) Let me put it another way. Billy Vroman's sister Olive threw a baseball better than I did.

But I have other reasons for not liking baseball, too. For one thing, the players all spit too much. Every time I try to watch a World Series game on television, someone's spitting at me. No game that can be played by a person with a wad of tobacco in his mouth is a sport.

Baseball has been called "The National Pastime." It's just the kind of game anyone deserves who has nothing better to do than try to pass his time. My own time is passing plenty fast enough without some national game to help it along.

What does "pastime" mean anyway? And why doesn't it have two "t"'s?

Maybe it's wishful thinking on my part but I think baseball is in trouble. It's been about ten years now since the President of the United States thought it was politically important for him to go throw out the first ball on opening day. All the balls are made in Haiti now, too, and most of the gloves are made in Taiwan.

It seems obvious to me that other sports are closing in on baseball and it's only a matter of time before the game will be squeezed out of the sports schedule. The professional basketball season doesn't end until a month after baseball starts, and football starts three months before baseball ends.

I don't like managers in sports either, and there is no other game where the manager is as important as in baseball. (I'll concede that a football coach has no business calling plays.) But what's managing got to do with a game? They sit in the dugout like little kings, waving, gesturing, spitting. They rush out on the field to challenge a decision by an umpire even though no decision has ever been changed in the hundred years the game has been played. When a manager storms out on the field, does he think this is going to be the first time? Why do they let the managers out on the field at all?

Managers are so important to the game of baseball that Little League has become a big deal for fathers. The kids would rather go hit a ball around a vacant lot or dodge cars playing baseball in the street, but that wasn't good enough for the manager-type fathers of America. They had to draw up a set of rules, have a regulation ball field made and see to it that the kids played on schedule. Never mind whether they felt like playing baseball that day or not. There's a schedule.

The Little League teams are sponsored by the local laundry or the gas station and, of course, the fathers are out there managing. The funny thing about all this is that we started playing the game in Taiwan after World War II and the American soldiers stationed there condescendingly offered to teach the Taiwanese kids how to play. You know what happened, of course. By the late 1960s, the kids in Taiwan were playing so well that they came over here and won the

Little League championship three years in a row. The "managers" of America rewrote the rules so Taiwan can't play in the Little League "World Championship" anymore.

Maybe they could get the President of Taiwan to throw out the first ball some year.

HOW TO WATCH FOOTBALL ON TELEVISION

Some of you don't like football. You have the mistaken notion that there's too much of it on television. This feeling can often be traced to the fact that you went to a college in the East where they actually let the students play on the team.

Well, of course there *is* quite a bit of football on television and it might be in order for me to suggest a few guidelines for watching it.

First, don't watch any pre-game shows.

Second, don't watch any post-game shows.

Third, don't watch any halftime shows. Try not to watch Howard Cosell at all. It's perfectly possible for anyone who knows the game to watch one without having anyone describe it to him.

For you casual football watchers who can take it or leave it, know which team you want to win. Find something about one of the teams you don't like and then root for the other team. It can be anything . . . you don't like the color of their uniforms . . . you once had a bad hotel room in the city the team represents . . . you've read where their middle linebacker is a dirty player or their quarterback is gay. Whatever it is, find something because an unreasonable prejudice against one of the teams is part of the satisfaction of watching football. It gets a lot of the hate out of your system.

People who don't like football don't understand people who do like it. There are some things these people ought to know. Remember this. The average football fan is a college graduate with an eighth-grade education. I, for instance, am a football fan. I'm a New York Giants fan and it hasn't always been easy. There have been times when I've thought about chucking it all in for ballet. I have a lucky Giant jacket I wear to the games, and some years I've worn it to eight home games and we've lost seven of them. How lucky can a jacket get?

There is something about being a football fan, though, that I recommend. Eight times a year, every home game, I make myself a tuna-fish sandwich, pour hot chicken broth in a vacuum bottle, put on some clothes too old to wear anyplace else and I take off for the game alone.

When I leave for the stadium, I don't have a care in the world. I have no encumbrances except my loyalty to a losing team. And if the Giants lose again this year and next, it won't make one damn bit of difference to my life.

I know that with all the games on television, a lot of you who don't like football but are basically good people anyway, are trying to understand those of us who do like football. You're trying to make some sense out of it. You see, that's where you're making your first mistake, right there. Being a football fan doesn't make *any sense at all* and that's the beauty of it.

POST SUPER BOWL 1980

Could I ask a little favor of some of you tonight? Please don't sit there saying you hate football and you're glad it's over. Don't say that. Some of us are very sad. There's a hole in our lives you could drive a truck through, as Frank Gifford might say.

Be kind to those of us who love football as we go through these agonizing weeks of withdrawal. Don't start out right away with saying cruel things. You know, things like, "You can unfasten your seat belt now, dear. The games are over." Or, "You remember your children, don't you? This is Donald. He turned nine while you were gone."

No one who has just lost a close friend wants to hear smart-aleck remarks. Just be patient and try to help us. We're going to be okay.

In another month or so, we'll be able to sit up and take food again at the dining-room table, instead of in front of the tube in the living room. We have a stack of Sunday papers we never got to read, but we have until next fall to catch up on them. Next fall starts with the first pre-season game on August 8th.

We'll be back in touch with the world again pretty soon, too. Pat Summerall mentioned Jimmy Carter during the halftime show a few weeks ago. He is still President, isn't he?

Be patient with us now that football's over.

GOOD NEWS

All of us who work in television news are constantly being accused of emphasizing the negative side of everything. We get letters saying we never cover a story unless something terrible happens.

Tonight we've put together a little news broadcast to give you an idea of how it would look if you had it your way.

"I'm here by the Mississippi. It's raining but the river is not overflowing its banks.

"As a matter of fact, it doesn't look to me as though there's any danger of a flood whatsoever. People are not piling up sandbags. No one has been forced to evacuate his home and the Governor has not asked that this be declared a federal disaster area."

"O'Hare Airport in Chicago is one of the nation's busiest. At 11 A.M., a jet aircraft with 168 passengers and ten crew members on board started down the long runway. The plane, headed for London, took off without incident. It landed without incident too. Everyone on board is now in London.

"One passenger on board that plane was quoted as saying he didn't like the fake milk they served with the coffee."

"For a report from New York City we take you to our correspondent standing in front of the Plaza, one of New York City's most luxurious hotels.

"This is the Plaza, one of New York City's most luxurious

hotels. CBS News has learned that last evening, after a night on the town, the Shah of Franakapan and his semi-beautiful wife returned to their hotel suite after depositing more than a million dollars' worth of jewelry in the hotel safe. The jewels included the famous Cooch Behar Diamond.

"This morning, when the safe was opened, all the jewelry including the famous Cooch Behar Diamond was right there where they'd left it."

"In Florida, the orange crop was hit by another night of average weather.

"The oranges just hung in there and grew."

"Oil industry officials announced today they were lowering prices because they just don't need the money. One reason for their affluence is their safety records.

"The oil tanks behind me are very close to a residential area. If they were on fire, smoke would be seen billowing up for miles around. They aren't on fire, though; they're just sitting there."

"In Detroit, a General Motors spokesman announced today that more than 174,000 Chevrolets made in the late fall of 1974 would not be recalled. They are all perfect.

"At eleven-thirty this evening, CBS News will present a special report listing the serial numbers of those cars."

And if that's what you want to hear, that's the way it was. Good evening.

JULY 4TH STATISTICS

One of the things we can be sure of over the July 4th weekend is that news reports will keep telling us how many of us are going to die in automobile accidents.

This weekend, for instance, they estimate there will be about 800 motor vehicle deaths. During the weekend, while you're driving, the radio makes your drive more pleasant by giving you the play-by-play account of the death statistics.

I was curious about the car death figures and how they fit into the total picture of our demise in America. The Department of Health, Education and Welfare keeps these day-to-day statistics for the country on how many people die and what they die of every day.

On the July 4th weekend in 1976, for instance, 758 people were killed in car crashes . . . a terrible figure. In April, the weekend comes on the same four days of the month and only 555 people were killed in cars.

But now here's the interesting thing about these figures. On those four days in April, a total of 21,700 people died of *all* causes. On the four days in July, 19,600 died—2,100 fewer. Not only that, 86 more people died in the four days right *after* the July 4th weekend than during it.

It turns out that Fourth of July is really quite a *safe* weekend for us.

There were 30 fewer suicides over the Fourth. In the four days in April, 156 people died in accidental falls. Twelve fewer fell to their deaths over the Fourth. On the Fourth, there were 75 murders; on the fourth of April, 77 murders. Fewer people are watching television over the Fourth, too, so I suppose fewer die of boredom.

But, overall, fewer of us die from all causes over the July 4th weekend than on most weekends.

This suggests two things. One, no matter what we do, whether we're climbing ladders or driving cars, a lot of people die doing it.

And, second, considering the number of people driving somewhere over the Fourth, the chances are that, car for car, it's one of the safest weekends of the year to be going someplace.

COUNTERS

I'm the all-American consumer. My idea of a good time is to go out Saturday morning to buy something with some of the money I've made. My comment here is about the counters I encounter in stores—you know, the place where you pay your money to the cashier.

If you go to one of those department stores where you have to pay on your way out, the little alley by the cashier is so camouflaged with goods that it's hard to find. You have to look for the line of people.

Why don't the stores give us a break and leave us a little room so we can put our packages down while we fish out our money? When you come to a counter with an armload of things you're buying, you want someplace to put them down. You never know how long you're going to have to stand there with them. Of course, the worst thing that can happen is when the person in front of you is paying by check.

We all know *why* they don't leave us any space. It's because they're always trying to sell us just one more item before we get out the door. They're trying to get us to buy razor blades, film, a magazine with Jackie Kennedy's picture on it, a pair of rubber gloves, maybe gum or candy for the kids.

It isn't only supermarkets and department stores, either. All kinds of stores make it hard for you to pay because there's no counter space. You have to poke your money through a crack in a wall of merchandise. If you drop your change, it often falls down in with the cigarettes. In some small stores, it's hard to find any counter space *at all*. And if you do find it, you can't see much of the person behind it taking the money.

Drugstores clutter their counters with little bottles and boxes of pills. Even liquor stores often hide their cash registers behind bottles of slow movers. It may be good for the liquor business, but it's a pain in the neck to the customer.

Often the counters at the delicatessen department are not only crowded with junk; they're so high you can't see over them at all. What are delicatessen departments hiding back there anyway? You don't really know what you've bought until you get it home and unwrap it.

My question is this: If they want us to buy, why don't they make it easier for us to pay?

IN PRAISE OF
NEW YORK CITY*

It's been popular in recent years to suggest that Nature is the perfect condition, that people have done nothing to the earth since they got here but make a mess of it. Well, that's true about some places but untrue about others.

New York City is as amazing in its own way as the Grand Canyon. As a matter of fact, you can't help thinking that maybe Nature would have made New York City look the way it does if it had had the money and the know-how.

When people talk about New York City, they usually mean the part of the city called Manhattan. Manhattan is a narrow rock island twelve miles long. Being an island is an important thing about New York because even though no one thinks much about it from day to day, they have to go to quite a bit of trouble to get on it and off it. This makes being there

*Broadcast February 1, 1974.

135

something of an event and people don't take it so lightly. New York isn't like so many places that just sort of dwindle away until you're out of town. In New York, it's very definite. You're either there or you aren't there.

The twenty-eight bridges and tunnels don't connect Manhattan with New Jersey and the four other boroughs. They're for entering and leaving New York. Where from or where to is of secondary importance. It may be some indication of the significance of the event that it costs $1.50 to cross the George Washington Bridge entering New York, nothing to cross leaving it.

The Brooklyn Bridge is a cathedral among bridges. Coming to Manhattan across it every morning is like passing through the Sistine Chapel on your way to work. You couldn't be going to an unimportant place.

Although two million people work on the little island, only half a million of those who work there live there. As a result, a million and a half people have to get on it every morning and off it every night. That's a lot of people to push through twenty-eight little tunnels and bridges in an hour or so, but it's this arterial ebb and flow that produces the rhythm to which this heartless city's heart beats. There must be something worth coming for when all those people go to that much trouble to get there.

Although it isn't the outstanding thing about it to the people who live or work there, New York is best known to strangers for what it looks like. And, of course, it looks tall.

The World Trade Center has two towers, each a quarter of a mile high. The New York office worker isn't overwhelmed by the engineering implications of flushing a toilet 106 floors above the street.

The buildings of the city are best seen from above, as though they were on an architect's easel. It's strange that they were built to look best from an angle at which hardly anyone ever sees them. From the street where the people are, you can't see the buildings for the city. The New Yorker doesn't worry about it because he never looks up.

You have to talk about tall buildings when you talk about New York, but to anyone who has lived for very long with both, the people of the city are of more continuing interest than the architecture. There is some evidence, of course, that the New Yorker isn't all that separate from his environment. If dogs and masters tend to look alike, so probably do cities and their citizens.

The New Yorker takes in New York air. For a short time it trades molecules with his bloodstream and he is part city. And then he exhales and the city is part him. They become inextricably mingled, and it would be strange if the people didn't come to look like the city they inhabit. And to some extent like each other.

While the rest of the nation feels fiercely about New York—they love it or they hate it—New Yorkers feel nothing. They use the city like a familiar tool. They don't defend it from love or hate. They shrug or nod in knowing agreement with almost anything anyone wants to say about it. Maybe this is because it's so hard to say anything about New York that isn't true.

New Yorkers don't brood much, either. They go about their business with a purposefulness that excludes introspection. If the rest of the country says New Yorkers lack pride because they have so little to be proud of, the New Yorker shrugs again. He has no argument with the South or the Midwest or Texas or California. He feels neither superior nor inferior. He just doesn't compare the things in New York with those anywhere else. He doesn't compare the subway with Moscow's or with the Métro in Paris. Both may be better, but neither goes to Brooklyn or Forest Hills and for this reason doesn't interest the New Yorker one way or the other.

New York is essentially a place for working but not everyone works in a glass cube. The island is crowded with highly individual nests people have made for themselves. There are 100,000 Waldens hidden in the stone and steel caverns.

The places people work and live are as different as the people. If a Hollywood façade is deceptive because it has nothing behind it, a New York façade is deceptive because it has so much. You can't tell much about what's inside from what you see outside. There are places within places. Houses behind houses. Very often in New York ugliness is only skin deep.

New York is the cultural center of mankind, too. Art flourishes in proximity to reality, and in New York the artist is never more than a stone's throw from the action. The pianist composes music three blocks from a fight in Madison Square Garden. A poet works against the sound of a jackhammer outside his window.

There are wonderfully good places to live in New York, if you have the money. A lot of New Yorkers *have* the money. Some of the grand old brownstones of an earlier era have been restored. There are no living spaces more comfortable anywhere. There are charming and unexpected little streets hidden in surprising places throughout the city. They attract

the artist, the actor, the musician. The insurance salesman lives on Long Island.

The city is crowded with luxury apartments, so even if you don't own your own brownstone, there's no need to camp out.

The average living place is an apartment built wall to wall with other apartments, so that they share the efficiency of water and electricity that flows to them through the same conduits. They're neither slums nor palaces.

If you can afford $2,500 a month for a three-bedroom apartment, you can live in a living room with Central Park as your front yard.

Several hundred thousand people do have Central Park for a front yard and it's certainly the greatest park on earth. It's a world of its own. No large city ever had the foresight to set aside such a substantial portion of itself to be one complete unbuilt-on place. It occupies 25 percent of the total area of Manhattan and yet any proposition to take so much as ten square feet of it to honor a Polish general or an American President brings out its legion of defenders.

There are crimes committed in the Park, but to say the Park is unsafe is like saying banks are unsafe because there are holdups. Life is unsafe, for that matter.

Most American cities have rotted from the center and the merchants have all moved to a place under one roof out in the middle of a suburban parking lot. Downtown was yesterday. New York is still vital at its core. It's the ultimate downtown. And if the biggest businesses are centered in New York so are the smallest.

Macy's, Gimbel's, Bloomingdale's are all here and so are the big grocery chains. But the place you probably buy your food is around the corner at a butcher's where you can still see both sides of a piece of meat.

If you want a rare and exotic cheese from Belgium, it's available or maybe you need a gear for a pump made in 1923.

All there somewhere in the city. If you're seven feet tall, there's a store that'll take care of you or they can fit you with pants if you have a waist that measures sixty-four inches. There's nothing you can't buy in New York if it's for sale anywhere in the world.

Money doesn't go as far in New York but it doesn't come as far, either. All the numbers for all the money in America are handled in Wall Street on lower Manhattan. The banks, the businesses and even the government do most of their money shuffling and dealing there.

If a civilization can be judged on its ability not only to

survive but to thrive in the face of natural obstacles, New York's civilization would have to be called among the most successful. For example, for what's supposed to be a temperate climate, New York has some of the most intemperate weather in the world. It's too hot in the summer, too cold in winter. During all its seasons, the wind has a way of whipping the weather at you and the rain is always coming from an angle that umbrella makers never considered.

The funny thing about it is that Nature and New York City have a lot in common. Both are absolutely indifferent to the human condition. To the New Yorker, accustomed to inconvenience of every kind, the weather is simply one more inconvenience.

New Yorkers learn young to proceed against all odds. If

something's in the way, they move it or go under it or over it or around it, but they keep going. There's no sad resignation to defeat. New Yorkers assume they can win. They have this feeling that they're not going to be defeated.

People talk as though they don't like crowds, but the crowd in New York bestows on the people it comprises a blessed anonymity. New Yorkers are protected from the necessity of being individuals when being one serves no purpose. This blending together that takes place in a crowd is a great time-saver for them.

New York can be a very private place too. There's none of the neighborliness based solely on proximity that dominates the lives you share your life with in a small town. It's quite possible to be not merely private but lonely in a crowd in New York. Loneliness seldom lasts, though. For one thing, troubles produce a warmth and comradeship like nothing else, and New York has so many troubles shared by so many people that there's a kind of common knowingness, even in evil, that brings them together. There is no one with troubles so special in New York that there aren't others in the same kind of trouble.

There are five thousand blind people making their way around the city. They're so much a part of the mix, so typical as New Yorkers, that they're treated with much the same hostile disregard as everyone else. Many of the blind walk through the city with the same fierce independence that moves other New Yorkers. They feel the same obligation to be all right. "I'm okay. I'm all right."

It might appear to any casual visitor who may have taken a few rides about town in a taxicab that all New Yorkers are filled with a loudmouthed ill will toward each other. The fact of the matter is, though, that however cold and cruel things seem on the surface, there has never been a society of people in all history with so much compassion for its fellowman. It clothes, feeds, and houses 15 percent of its own because 1.26 million people in New York are unable to do it for themselves. You couldn't call that cold or cruel.

Everyone must have seen pictures at least of the great number of poor people who live in New York. And it seems strange, in view of this, that so many people come here seeking their fortune or maybe someone else's. But if anything about the city's population is more impressive than the great number of poor people, it's the great number of rich people. There's no need to search for buried treasure in New York. The great American dream is out in the open for everyone to see and to reach for. No one seems to resent the very rich. It must be because even those people who can never realistically believe they'll get rich themselves can still dream about it. And they respond to the hope of getting what they see others having. Their hope alone seems to be enough to sustain them. The woman going into Tiffany's to buy another diamond pin can pass within ten feet of a man without money enough for lunch. They are oblivious to each other. He feels no envy; she no remorse.

There's a disregard for the past in New York that dismays even a lot of New Yorkers. It's true that no one pays much attention to antiquity. The immigrants who came here came for something new, and what New York used to be means nothing to them. Their heritage is somewhere else.

Old million-dollar buildings are constantly being torn down and replaced by new fifty-million-dollar ones. In London, Rome, Paris, much of the land has only been built on once in all their long history. In relatively new New York, some lots have already been built on four times.

Because strangers only see New Yorkers in transit, they leave with the impression that the city is one great mindless rush to nowhere. They complain that it's moving too fast, but they don't notice that it's getting there first. For better and for

worse, New York has *been* where the rest of the country is going.

The rest of the country takes pride in the legend on the Statue of Liberty: ''Give me your tired, your poor,/Your huddled masses.../The wretched refuse of your teeming shore....'' Well, for the most part it's been New York City, not the rest of the country, that took in those huddled masses.

Millions of immigrants who once arrived by ships stopped off in New York for a generation or two while the city's digestive system tried to assimilate them before putting them into the great American bloodstream. New York is still trying to swallow large numbers of immigrants. They don't come by boat much anymore and they may not even be from a foreign country. The influx of a million Puerto Ricans in the 1960s produced the same kind of digestive difficulties that the influx of the Irish did in the middle 1800s.

New York's detractors, seeing what happens to minority groups, have said there is just as much prejudice here as anywhere. New York could hardly deny that. The working whites hate the unemployed blacks. The blacks hate the whites. The Puerto Ricans live in a world of their own. The Germans, the Hungarians, the Poles live on their own blocks. Nothing in this pot has melted together. The Chinese and the Italians live side by side in lower Manhattan as though Canal Street was the Israeli border. There's no intermingling, and in a city with almost two million Jews even a lot of *Jews* are anti-Semitic.

In spite of it all, the city works. People do get along. There is love.

Whether New York is a pleasure or a pain depends on what it is you wish to fill your life with. Or whether you wish to fill it at all. There is an endless supply of satisfaction available to anyone who wishes to help himself to it. It's not an easy city, but the cups of its residents runneth over with life.

It's a city of extremes. There's more of everything. The range of notes is wider. The highs are higher. The lows lower. The goods, the bads are better and worse. And if you're unimpressed by statistics, consider the fact that in 1972 the cops alone in New York City were charged with stealing $73 million worth of heroin. There are 1,700 murders in an average year.

Neither of those statistics is so much a comment on crime as it is a comment on the size and diversity of New York City.

No one keeps a statistic on Life. The probability is that, like everything else, there's more of it in New York.

THE DRAFT

The argument about the draft is pretty dull because there are only two issues involved. One, should we have a draft at all? And two, if we have one, should we draft women?

The President could have considered a lot of other alternatives that would have made the argument more interesting, it seems to me. For instance, a sixteen-year-old boy wrote a letter to my hometown newspaper suggesting drafting *only* women. Well, now, *there's* an idea for you.

Men have been discriminated against in the draft for more than two hundred years. Maybe we ought to start an affirmative-action program, draft nothing but women until the total number of women drafted equals the total number of men who have ever been drafted. Even West Point would be all women with maybe eight or ten token men, just enough for an occasional newspaper feature story about how they're doing there.

Keep in mind, no one is saying men shouldn't serve in the Army at all. Far from it. There are certain noncombat jobs men are especially well qualified to do. Men make good medics, for example, because they're kinder, gentler, more sympathetic to someone in trouble. I think it would be safe to say that basically they're nicer people.

Wouldn't a proposition like that make the draft argument more interesting? Or how about using our free-enterprise system to attract people to the service? Offer to pay privates $50,000 a year, but only take the best applicants. There'd be plenty of applicants. This way we'd get good people and the Army and Navy wouldn't have to be so big.

There's more to the idea. Everyone wants to be an officer, no one wants to be a private, so privates would be paid the highest salary. As soon as a private was made a corporal, he'd only make *$40,000* a year. A sergeant would make $35,000, and so on. By the time anyone in the Army got to be a general, she'd only be making $7,500 a year, something like that. There are *always* plenty of people who want to be the general.

Here's another idea. What about limiting the draft to people between the ages of fifty and sixty? A lot of us are in better shape now than we were when we were twenty and we're a lot smarter, too. Now, some fifty-year-olds might protest against registering for the draft, but wouldn't it be a relief to see someone other than *students* protesting for a change?

There are so many possibilities. What would you think about just drafting cigarette smokers? The ones who smoke more than a pack a day would serve in combat at the front lines, because . . . well, you know.

Well, something to argue about, isn't it?

POLITICAL PARTIES

A lot of you probably aren't sure whether you're Republicans or Democrats. We have an election coming up shortly, and you ought to find out what you are. I thought it might help if I explained the difference between Republicans and Democrats.

Democrats believe the trouble started with Herbert Hoover, and was worse during the Presidency of Richard Nixon.

Republicans believe the trouble started with Franklin Roosevelt, and is worse than ever right now.

Democrats leave the dishes in the drying rack on the sink overnight.

Republicans put the dishes away every night.

Republicans play tennis.

Democrats bowl, unless they're Kennedy Democrats, in which case they play tennis too.

Democrats love television, and watch a lot of it.
Republicans hate television. They watch a lot of it too.

Democrats are baseball fans.
Republicans follow college football.

Democrats buy their food on payday once a week at the supermarket.
Republicans go to the grocery store every day.

Democrats usually write with a pencil.
Republicans use pens.

In the summer, Democrats drink beer.
Republicans drink gin and tonic. In the winter, they drink Scotch and soda.
Democrats drink beer.

Republicans think taxes are too high because of the Democrats.
Democrats think taxes are too high because of the Republicans.

Republicans have dinner between seven and eight.
Democrats have supper between five and six.

Democrats drink coffee with cream and sugar, from mugs.
Republicans take theirs black—with cup and saucer.

Democrats don't seal the envelopes of their Christmas cards, which they sign by hand.
Republicans seal the envelopes of their Christmas cards, which have their names printed on them—unless they're very

rich Republicans, in which case they sign them by hand. If they're very, very rich, they have someone else sign them.

Democrats believe people are basically good but must be saved from themselves by their government.

Republicans believe people are basically bad but they'll be okay if they're left alone.

A lot of Republicans are more like Democrats used to be, and a lot of Democrats are more like Republicans used to be. If you're still not sure what you are, you're probably a Democrat.

HOW WE ELECT
THE PRESIDENT

Most of us know how we elect our President, of course. It's a
very simple democratic process. All it is is every American
citizen over the age of eighteen votes for whomever he or she
wants. That's all there is to it—practically all. There are a
few little details.

For instance, first the voters pick the two people they want
to run against each other, two outstanding Americans. This
year it looks as though it'll be an old movie actor and a
former peanut farmer.

Actually the voters don't choose those people, the members
of the political parties do. It's called the primary system. The
first primary is held in New Hampshire in February because
it's—well, it doesn't matter *why* it's held there then, but it is.

So, beginning with New Hampshire, the two parties pick a
candidate. They *sort* of pick a candidate. What really happens
is they pick the delegates who will go to their party's

convention. The delegates have to vote for the candidate the party members want them to—or at least in some states they have to. In other states, the delegates picked can vote for anybody they want to once they get to the convention. Then these thoughtful, handpicked Americans, who represent the whole country, solemnly decide who they want.

I think you can see how simple this system is that we have for electing our President. Once the candidates are chosen by the two parties, that's about it . . . unless, of course, there's a third party.

Now then, on November 4th all Americans go to the polls and vote for their choice. The person who gets the majority of the votes is President. That's *just about* it, anyway. The fact is, only about 54 percent of all Americans eligible to vote voted last time and the election was close, so you have to cut that figure in two, so only about 28 percent of us really voted to make Jimmy Carter President.

It doesn't matter, though, because the voters don't elect a President directly anyway. Actually they're voting for *representatives* among the 538 people in the electoral college. They are the ones who *actually* vote to elect our President.

The people in the electoral college are chosen—well, they're chosen a lot the way New Hampshire was chosen to be the first primary state.

Let me read to you from the Constitution on how that works. It's called "Present Mode of Electing President and Vice-President by Electors." "The electors shall meet in their respective states and vote by ballot for President and Vice-President, one of whom, at least, shall not be an inhabitant of the same state with themselves."

". . . one of whom shall not be an inhabitant of the same state with themselves."

Well, that's how we elect our President. Trust me.

POLLS

You'll all be excited to learn that the results of the latest poll are in and I have them for you right here.

First you ought to know a little about the poll. The poll is about polls. It was prepared by me and I asked the questions of a broad cross section of nine Americans who work in the same office as I do.

Our first question was this, in two parts: In your opinion, which of the following polls are dullest and least accurate? Louis Harris/ABC, Gallup, Roper, CBS News/New York Times or NBC/Associated Press?

Seven of those polled thought they were all dull. Thirty-four percent said they thought the first two were most accurate *least* often. Fifty-six percent said that the last three were least accurate *most* often.

Second question: If the polls indicated that 90 percent of all Americans thought President Carter was doing a bad job, would you be more likely to vote for Teddy Kennedy?

Forty percent said "Maybe yes, Maybe no." Twenty-nine percent were undecided. Eleven percent said they didn't understand the question.

The remaining 22 percent said they'd rather have the Ayatollah Khomeini than Teddy Kennedy for President.

Third question: On Election Day the winners are often announced by the networks before the voting booths are closed. Does this lessen or increase your interest in voting?

Forty-one percent said "Yes." The rest of those polled said that if predicting was an exact science, weathermen wouldn't be wrong so often.

Fourth question: Have you ever been polled, has anyone in your immediate family ever been polled and do you care whether you're ever polled again? The answers to this question suggest some of those questioned weren't paying attention.

Twenty-three percent said "Walter Cronkite." Fifty-one percent said "Would you please repeat the question?" The rest told us to get lost.

Our last question was this: Even if the polls are accurate, do you wish they'd stop taking them? Here are the answers to that question:

"Yes," 50 percent. "No," 50 percent. "Undecided," 50 percent.

There's a margin for error on a question like this of about 50 percent one way or the other.

Finally, our poll indicated that if the next Presidential election were to be held this week, the winner would be the American public. It would save us all a lot of time and money.

DEBATES

Tonight's debate between the Presidential candidates won't be the only one, and I think it might be a good idea and make them more interesting if each of us kept a scorecard. I've drawn up a sample scorecard here. What you do is you give each candidate a mark of from zero to ten in each category.

APPEARANCE, for example. Give each candidate the score you think he should have for his appearance. If he doesn't appear at all, of course, he gets a zero.

INFLATION. From what they've said, how well do you think they'll handle inflation? You might also take into consideration whether the candidate sounds a little inflated himself.

NECKTIE. You'd want to consider color, how much you think it cost, how well it was tied and whether you think the candidate tied it himself or had a makeup person do it.

STALLING. Score them on whether or not they were evasive during the debate. If a candidate used a lot of phrases like "I think my position is clear on that," instead of saying what his position is, you'd give him a low mark.

ERA. ABORTION. GUN CONTROL. This is just one category here because they're the same thing. Everyone who is against one is against the others, and vice versa.

ENERGY. DEFENSE. HAIR. Reagan and Anderson both have good-looking hair. You might want to give them each an eight, unless you think Reagan dyes his brown; then you might want to give him only a two. If you think Anderson dyes his gray, give him a ten.

STANDABILITY. This is a difficult category, but it's important. You know how it is with some candidates? No matter what they say, you can't stand them. Mark them from zero to ten on standability.

So that's it. I've got just one more idea for the last debate. We'll all know what the candidates think by then, and we are, after all, electing a First Lady, too. So the last debate will be different. For half an hour, each candidate will argue with his wife.

POLLS 1980

The election's long over, of course, and Ronald Reagan's been declared the winner. He got 43 million votes and Carter only got 35 million. But I'm still waiting to see who the *polltakers* say won the election. I mean, votes don't mean anything because they aren't scientific, like polls are.

I kept a file of a lot of poll stories over the past year. You probably read some of them.

"REPUBLICAN, INDEPENDENT VOTERS PICK FORD IN POLL"— Louis Harris. This was taken before the Republican Convention. Obviously, Gerald Ford was going to be the Republican candidate.

In August, "AP–NBC POLL SHOWS PREZ GAINING SHARPLY ON RON." This was before most of us even knew he was behind.

Time magazine's poll in September had them even at 39 percent.

According to Mervin Field, Reagan's lead in California

began to shrink in September. He only won by 1.4 million votes in California.

"CARTER LEADS REAGAN IN ILLINOIS, POLL SAYS"—Carter 27 percent, Reagan 23 percent. The Chicago *Tribune* thought Carter was leading in Illinois, but admitted that 35 percent of the voters hadn't decided who to vote for yet. Apparently, 90 percent of the 35 percent decided to vote for Reagan.

In October, Carter was narrowing the gap in Virginia, according to the Richmond *Times-Dispatch*.

At the same time, he was gaining again in the ABC/Harris poll: Reagan 49 percent, Carter 46 percent. Carter sure did a lot of gaining in the polls.

The same day, the CBS/New York Times poll had Carter pulling even at 39 percent. They made it all very clear with a chart: "Carter found clear favorite among evangelicals." I always wondered, if you're born again do you get to vote twice?

Toward the end, they were all saying the race was about even. I took a little post-election poll myself. I asked one question of four people around the office. I asked them, "If the election was today, would you vote the same way you did?"

One person said he would; one person said he wouldn't; one person said he always got so confused in the voting booth that he couldn't remember who he'd voted for. The fourth person said she voted for Anderson and she'd do it again, too, because no matter what happens now, it isn't her fault.

I think all the polls this year make one thing very clear: the election was a lot closer than the unscientific voting would indicate.

THE CAPITAL

Someone has written in suggesting we move the nation's capital out of Washington to somewhere in Kansas because that's closer to the center of the country. It's an old idea, but it might be worth considering.

If you've ever moved out of a house or an office, you know you have to go through all your old junk, and you end up throwing half of it away. There's no place on earth that needs stuff thrown away like Washington does.

The Capitol itself is a grand old building. We should certainly keep that. It could be taken down at its present location and put back up again in a wheat field in Kansas. Most of the big buildings we could leave. There's no need to take all those departments, agencies, bureaus and committees to Kansas. No need to take the Treasury Building, for instance. The Treasury is $790 billion in debt. Why take a building with nothing in it?

No need to take the Supreme Court Building either, I think. It's beautiful for a reporter to stand in front of, but it has a cold look. I think the Supreme Justices would seem less remote from all of us if they made their decisions from maybe rocking chairs on a comfortable front porch in Kansas.

The next question is this: What do we do with Washington? It's too good to throw away. The idea I like is to make Washington into one huge tourist-attracting Disneyland. It really wouldn't be much of a change.

The Pentagon could become a fun house. It's already a wonderful place to get lost in just as it is. Visitors could spend many happy hours playing in the Pentagon halls. The White House would be unchanged, except that the Presidents and their families would be represented by moving models—perhaps featuring a different Presidential family on each day of the month.

If we leave the old White House in Washington, of course, we'll need a new one in Kansas. Well, the President's always traveling around the country. Maybe the new White House should be a mobile home. That way, no matter where he went the President would know where his pajamas were.

MR. ROONEY GOES TO WASHINGTON*

People want to know what's going on in Washington. Last year 19 million Americans went there trying to find out. They spent most of their time lined up outside some place. The trouble with that is, like tourists anywhere, they leave no smarter about the place than they were when they came.

Several months ago CBS sent me to Washington to see what a nonpolitical reporter with no previous knowledge of that place could find out about it. It was a good assignment, like spending two months as a tourist in a foreign country with the company paying the bill.

The first thing I did in Washington was to try to find my way around. It's all right to say you're going to do some investigating, but it's embarrassing the first day when you go out the door and don't know whether to turn left or right to get to the White House.

---

*Broadcast January 26, 1975.

I spent several days just looking around and taking pictures. No one can stand being a tourist for long, though, and the things I wanted to find out about Washington were the things the guidebooks don't tell you.

Two and three-quarters million people are paid $35 billion a year to work for the federal government. I keep trying to find out exactly why it is our government has grown so big and why there are so many bureaus in the bureaucracy.

One of the reasons seems to be that almost every committee, every agency or every department is established by law, but there is never anything in that law about putting the agency out of business when its job is done. Once established, a government agency, like a government job, is practically immortal. If a committee or agency has a name that makes it sound out-of-date, it doesn't go out of business; it just changes its name.

We kept asking people if what they were doing was really necessary or if it was something the government ought to be doing for us in the first place.

We thought maybe Civil Defense was something out-of-date that we could do without. We had a nice talk with the Director of Civil Defense, John E. Davis.

The first thing we found out was, it isn't called that anymore.

DAVIS:

Two years ago we changed our name to Defense Civil Preparedness Agency. We wanted to be more inclusive, to look at natural disasters as well as preparation against survival from a nuclear attack.

ROONEY:

People say that you're an agency in search of a mission.

DAVIS:

Quite to the contrary. This organization has taken on a

currency role and I refer to the natural disasters that we have frequently occurring in practically all sections of the United States. There's none that escapes . . . tornadoes, hurricanes, earthquakes, winter storms. . . .

ROONEY:

I'm confused about the Office of Emergency Preparedness in relation to you. Is there any overlapping there?

DAVIS:

We are the Office of—Oh, Office of Emergency Preparedness? Of course, that was a year ago in July, by Executive Order. It was separated and part of it now, of the Office of Emergency Preparedness, is called Office of Preparedness, which is in GSA, responsible generally for the continuity of government and certain emergency plans that were, had been associated with OEP. And part of it, the disaster relief generally, FDAA, Federal Disaster Assistance Agency, is over in HUD. And they administer the rehabilitation and have some responsibilities for assisting states as we do, but we have been assigned the mission of helping local communities prepare for these natural disasters. And that generally is where we get the authorities for what we're doing in the natural disaster field.

ROONEY:

We've been looking at some of your literature that you've been publishing and we're particularly interested in this one, *Protecting Mobile Homes from High Winds*. Is telling people how to protect their mobile homes from tipping over a function of government?

DAVIS:

It's just one of these things that was done because of our professional knowledge and the fact that it was something that people wanted today.

ROONEY:

I was taken with this one phrase in here. "Mobile homes

173

meet a real need in our society: they are attractive, comfortable, and provide low-cost housing.'' Now, for a government booklet to say mobile homes are attractive . . . I never heard anybody call a mobile home attractive before.

DAVIS:

Well, it's—

ROONEY:

Why would a government booklet call a mobile home attractive?

DAVIS:

Well, I think that this is a matter of opinion. Certainly the manufacturers of mobile homes and I imagine those that live in it—to them that is the case. And so it's all a relative thing.

ROONEY:

What is your budget, your total budget?

DAVIS:

Eighty-two million dollars last year and it appears that it's under consideration by the Congress now and I think it will be approximately the same amount.

With the draft over, I thought our government might be saving money by closing the Selective Service Agency. We talked to the Director, Byron Pepitone, a retired Air Force colonel. We asked him what Selective Service was doing now that it wasn't selecting anyone anymore.

PEPITONE:

We have become an organization in standby . . . much as an organization in the sense of insurance against an emergency. We're not inducting anyone, you see. The authority to do so has expired. But our staff and our offices have been reduced by a quarter, by three-quarters.

ROONEY:

How much is your budget?

PEPITONE:

In the spring of 1973, before inductions stopped, we were operating on a budget of approximately a hundred million dollars. Our request to the Congress for the fiscal year '75 forthcoming will be for forty-seven million dollars.

ROONEY:

Is that the absolute minimum that it costs to do *nothing?* Not to draft *anyone?*

PEPITONE:

Forty-seven million dollars is a very small amount to guarantee that should you have to augment that force, you have the capacity to do it in a timely fashion.

ROONEY:

What would happen to your operation if you spent only twenty million?

PEPITONE:

Well, my personal opinion is that if it gets much below the present level, we might just as well decide that we don't need it.

It's hard to show the size of government. It isn't as though you could get everyone who works for it to pose for one big class picture. And, of course, it hasn't always been this big, either.

In 1930, half of all government employees were mailmen. Now there are a lot more mailmen, but they represent only 25 percent of all government workers.

And back then, there was no such thing as a Department of Health, Education and Welfare. Our health, education and welfare were pretty much our own business. Well, of course, things have changed. Today, there are 127,000 HEW employ-

ees. The agency occupies space in fifty-seven buildings in the Washington area alone.

We thought it would be interesting to find out how many government buildings there are in the Washington area. We asked the General Services Administration for a complete list. They told us they didn't have one, but they could get us one for $150.

So we paid them $150 and here's the list they gave us. *(A computer printout unravels to the floor.)* This is a list of every government building in the Washington area.

I have another printout, too: ''Real Property Owned by the United States.'' It's a list of every building our government owns all over the world. The CIA may have a pad or two in Budapest that isn't listed here, but substantially these are our real-estate holdings. Something like half a million buildings. Our government owns them.

The General Services Administration is an interesting operation. What it is, is a combination landlord and superintendent for all government buildings. If you work for the government and need a whole new building or just a box of rubber bands, you go to the General Services Administration.

Now, this is their catalog (*holding it up*). About anything you'd want is in here, and there are quite a few things you wouldn't want, too.

Here's a chair. They have sixteen different kinds of chairs, for instance. There are eighteen grades of government servants, so I suppose there's one chair for each grade . . . The bottom two grades must have to stand.

Here are the rubber bands, if you want rubber bands. This one here is Federal Specification ZZR001415. So the government's got just about everything you want if you work for it.

We wondered where all this stuff in the catalog came from so we went out to one of the General Services warehouses to look around.

(*Examining conveyor belt*) What would you like? Here's boxes of leather gloves. Mops. I imagine the mop handles will be coming along. Some kind of lock. String. There are two balls—for toilet bowls? A couple of dictionaries. You want a dictionary? Pans, pots, wrenches.

What would you like? Nameplates for executives' desks. Here's paint rollers. And where would the government be without—you thought this was a figure of speech—genuine government red tape.

I don't think there's anything more discouraging for a taxpayer who likes to think that he's doing something important for his country than to see something like this. You look at one of these boxes on the conveyor belt and you say to yourself, "There go my taxes . . . not democracy or freedom or a battleship or anything . . . just a box of stuff."

This chart, "Pay System Total General Schedule," shows all the ranks of Civil Service workers in government. There are eighteen grades and there are ten steps within each grade too, but we're not going to get into that.

And we aren't going to get into double-dipping either. In Washington, double-dipping is the practice of retiring from the Army, Navy or Air Force and then taking a job in Civil Service so that you get two salaries.

There are more government workers in Grade 5 than any other, 172,000. Each of them makes the minimum of $9,000. And it costs the government a billion and a half.

Grades 16, 17 and 18 all make $36,000. You'll see that Grade 16 is listed at thirty-five five, but actually Grade 16 makes $36,000 too . . . after he's been in the government for about twenty minutes.

It's one of the problems in government. All three top grades make the same, so there's not much advantage to getting to be the boss . . . except possibly you get to go home a little early on Friday.

If Civil Service worked the way it's supposed to work, it would be fine. It's supposed to go like this: If someone needs a certain kind of employee, he goes to his department's employment office and they find someone in their card file who fits his job description.

According to the people we talked to, it doesn't work ideally very often, though. Something like this is more apt to happen: Say I'm in a management position in government. I have a job open. My old college roommate needs a job but the description of the job in my office doesn't match his qualifications. He worked in the real-estate business for a while. He had a job in a bank once. His father is Italian. And he was editor of our college newspaper.

I want to help my old roommate, so I get him to apply to Civil Service. He puts down all his qualifications.

A short while later, I go to Civil Service and I say, "Say, that job I have is changed. What I need now is someone with newspaper experience to help our office with some real-estate dealings in an Italian neighborhood. He should have knowledge of mortgages and bank loans."

So someone at Civil Service takes that information, feeds it into a computer and, presto, guess whose name pops up? My old college roommate's.

The Civil Service payroll represents only half of what the government pays out in salaries every year, though. The names in a book called *United States Government Policy and Supporting Positions* represent something else. These are the people who work for government but are not Civil Service. In other words, these people were all appointed to their jobs.

This thing really makes good reading, too. Look at some of the titles in here:

—SECRETARY TO THE SECRETARY
—SECRETARIAL ATTENDANT TO THE SECRETARY
—CHAUFFEUR TO THE SECRETARY

Apparently the chauffeur doesn't have a secretary himself.
And then there are all the confidential people:

—CONFIDENTIAL STAFF ASSISTANT
—CONFIDENTIAL STAFF ASSISTANT TO THE ASSOCIATE DIRECTOR
—CONFIDENTIAL ASSISTANT
—CONFIDENTIAL STAFF ASSISTANT.

Secretary to the Secretary	Associate Deputy Administrator
Secretarial Attendant to the Secretary.	Deputy Associate Administrator
Chauffeur to the Secretary	Associate Administrator for Procurement and Management Assistance.
	Special Assistant to Associate Administrator for Procurement and Management Assistance.

Confidential Staff Assistant to Associate Director, Human Rights.	Deputy Assistant Secretary
Congressional Relations Specialist	Special Assistant to the Assistant Secretary.
Confidential Assistant	Staff Assistant to the Deputy Assistant Secretary.
do	Private Secretary to the Assistant Secretary.
Policy Analyst	Private Secretary to the Deputy Assistant Secretary.
Congressional Relations Specialist	
Confidential Assistant to Assistant Director for P.R. & E.	
Confidential Secretary to the Director.	Assistant Administrator for Administration.
Confidential Assistant to Special Assistant to Director.	Deputy Assistant Administrator for Administration.
Confidential Assistant to the Director.	
Confidential Staff Assistant.	
Confidential Staff Assistant to the Associate Director, Congressional Relations.	
Confidential Assistant	Confidential Assistant (Private Secretary) to the Secretary of Labor.
do	Assistant to Special Assistant to Secretary, Office of Legislative Liaison.
Confidential Staff Assistant	
Private Secretary (Stenography) OEO Director.	
Confidential Assistant	Special Assistant to the Secretary
Confidential Staff Assistant	do
Confidential Staff Assistant to Assistant Director.	Special Assistant to the Director, Federal Contract Compliance.
Confidential Staff Assistant to Assistant Director.	Assistant to Special Assistant to Secretary, Office of Legislative Liaison.
Confidential Assistant to the Associate Director Congressional Relations.	Special Assistant to the Secretary
Confidential Staff Assistant	Assistant to the Special Assistant to the Secretary for Communications.
Confidential Secretary to the Director.	Assistant to Special Assistant to Secretary, Office of Legislative Liaison.
Confidential Staff Assistant	Special Assistant to the Secretary
Confidential Secretary to the Special Assistant.	
Confidential Secretary (Stenography)	
Confidential Secretary	
Confidential Secretary to Associate Director, Congressional Relations	
Confidential Assistant to Special Assistant to Director	
Confidential Secretary (Stenography)	
Confidential Secretary	
Confidential Secretary to the Deputy Director.	

Confidential, confidential, confidential . . . In Washington, a confidential assistant is the person who, if you don't want to know something, you go and ask him and he won't tell you.

There are also some beauties here:

—ASSOCIATE DEPUTY ADMINISTRATOR

—DEPUTY ASSOCIATE ADMINISTRATOR

And down further:

—DEPUTY ASSISTANT SECRETARY

—SPECIAL ASSISTANT TO THE ASSISTANT SECRETARY

—STAFF ASSISTANT TO THE DEPUTY ASSISTANT SECRETARY
—ASSISTANT ADMINISTRATOR FOR ADMINISTRATION
—DEPUTY ASSISTANT ADMINISTRATOR FOR ADMINISTRATION
And it goes on like that.

Government officials are always saying there aren't any more federal employees now than there were twenty years ago. This sounds good until you find out what the reason is.

The reason is an awful lot of government work in Washington is being done by private companies now, on contract.

I grew up thinking big government and big business were enemies. Well, imagine how surprised I was to find out they're really best friends . . . very close buddies. As a matter of fact, in Washington big business and big government get along so well it scares the life out of you.

The Department of Defense, for instance, has 80,000 people on its payroll who arrange contracts with private companies who actually do the work. There are hundreds of companies in Washington which do nothing but advise the government.

Here's a little example we looked into . . . a report on urban mass transportation presented by the Secretary of the Department of Transportation to the President of the Senate. At the time it was Gerald Ford. The letter accompanying the report says:

Dear Mr. President:

I am pleased to submit the Department's study of Urban Mass Transportation, needs and financing, etc.

Sincerely,
Claude S. Brinegar
Sec. Dept. Transportation

Well, now, you'd think this had been prepared by the Department of Transportation, wouldn't you? It wasn't. It was prepared by a private company called Peat, Marwick and Mitchell.

We got hold of the contract under which Peat, Marwick did this study. They were paid $260,564 for it. Would anyone know the study was done by Peat, Marwick? Would the Senate or the public know? Not from anything you could find in this study, because Peat, Marwick and Mitchell's name isn't mentioned anywhere in it. Not even in fine print.

The trouble with contracting is that it makes it even harder for all of us to find out where our money is going.

We tried for months to get someone at Peat, Marwick and Mitchell to talk to us about this. They refused. What are they hiding? There's no law they have to talk to us, of course, but, well, it *is* our money.

One of the obvious problems is that when a private company gives advice to the government in some special area and also has private clients in that *same* area, it seems very unlikely that the advice they give the government will do their *private* clients any harm.

Here's another example of contracting. We were looking through the *Commerce Business Daily* one day. I never heard of the publication before, but it's important to people in Washington doing business with the government. It lists contracts up for bids, contracts let, that sort of thing. We came on one small contract that had been given out. It said what the company was supposed to do: "Prepare guideline to be used for the rewriting of all Navy technical manuals to the ninth grade level."

A company called Biotechnology got the contract and were to be paid $65,622. Now that seemed interesting, so we set out trying to find out more about it.

First, we called Biotechnology. We didn't get far.

(*On phone*) "Andy Rooney, CBS News. Rooney, R-O-O-N-E-Y. . . . Well, check with him, will you, and see if he'll talk with me. . . . He's not there right now, huh? Do you think he went somewhere? Is he apt to be in again today?"

(I'm always amazed at how a secretary can sit three feet from a guy and not know whether he's in or not.)

"Oh, you don't think he'll be back today. All right, put me on hold, fine. . . . I've been on hold before. . . . Out of the building, eh?"

(She's asking him whether he's in or not, I think.)

"What time is he apt to be in, do you know? Do you know what time he's apt to be in? . . . Around eleven . . . okay. Well, do you think if I call him around . . . He may go right to lunch from . . . instead of coming in at eleven. That's an early lunch. Do you know whether he has a lunch appointment or where he would be going? Will he call in and let you know whether he's coming in or not? . . . He wouldn't let you know about that. . . . And if he's *not* coming in, he won't tell you? Okay. Well, why don't I try you again at eleven then, and see if you know anything. . . ."

Several days later, much to our surprise, we got through to the company's president.

(On phone) "Andy Rooney, CBS News. How are you? I've been trying to get you for a long while. Would you be able to tell me, you know, who you're dealing with in the Navy? Is that a secret? *(Listens)* I just wondered, you know, if you could talk to us on camera someday about how it goes and what you do and that sort of thing? . . .

"Well, is the Navy apt to say they don't want any publicity at all on it? If you can get approval from the Navy, we could talk on camera. *(Listens)* Well, would you check it with them or should I?"

They told me they couldn't talk about it without Navy permission. So we went to the Navy. You haven't *seen* red tape until you deal with the Navy. We talked to them . . . a lot of them.

(On phone) "I was just trying to find out, you know, what was happening, what the Navy was doing with their manuals. . . .

"I had been trying to talk with some people at a company named Biotechnology. Are you familiar with them? . . . Yeah. I . . . you know, it just doesn't seem like anything very sneaky to me. I don't see why they wouldn't talk about it. They were reluctant to talk until they had gotten some sort of clearance from you people at the Navy.

"I then talked to a Mr. Shihda, and he referred me to a Mr. Tarbell, and Mr. Tarbell referred me to Mr. Cleverly. And then I guess he referred me to you. Do you think there would be any objection to my talking to the people at Biotech? . . . All right, thanks a lot, okay."

After weeks of phone calls, we reached someone in the Navy who said it was all right to talk to Biotechnology about it . . . if it was all right with them.

You won't be surprised to learn that Biotechnology still refused to talk to me.

We were really interested now and we were able to get hold of the Navy study on which that contract was based: *"Navy Enlisted Occupational Classification System (NEOCS) Study, Volume II."* Armed with this study, we went to the Navy and had an interview with Admiral Frederick Palmer, the man in charge of implementing it.

ROONEY:

Are you having all the manuals rewritten to a ninth-grade level of comprehension, Admiral?

PALMER:

I think that needs a little explanation, because I think that you need to go further and find out ninth grade according to what standard.

ROONEY:

Has this contract been executed yet?

PALMER:

No.

ROONEY:

They haven't done the work?

PALMER:

No.

ROONEY:

We had tried to contact Biotechnology. Do you know Biotechnology?

PALMER:

No, I do not.

ROONEY (aside):

It just seems strange to us that the officer in charge of implementing this study never heard of Biotechnology or of the chart on page 51, dividing all potential Navy enlistees into four categories.

ROONEY (to Admiral):

I saw a report and it divided Navy enlistees into four categories: Socially Assertive Team Leaders; Uninvolved Reward Seekers; Active Manual Satisfaction Seekers; and Unrealistic Self-Improvement Seekers. You recognize them in the Navy?

PALMER:

I haven't the foggiest notion of what you're talking about. I hope I can get a copy of that to look into.

ROONEY:

Wasn't that in Volume II of your study?

PALMER:

I don't recall that at all.

ROONEY:

I think it was.

PALMER:

Do you have the page number of that?

ROONEY:

No, I don't. It was known as the Grey study.

PALMER:

I'll sure look it up. I'll make a note of that right now.

ROONEY:

If you had your report with you, I think it's probably in there.

PALMER:

Grey study. Volume II, you say. Thank you.

We're not drawing any conclusions about the Navy or this little company. They're probably both fine, but these contracts sure make it difficult for a citizen to find out where $65,000 goes.

And keep in mind that contract was only one of 583 that appeared in the *Commerce Business Daily* that day alone. We didn't have time to check the other 582.

Having struck out at both Peat, Marwick and Mitchell and Biotechnology, we went to a company called McKinsey.

McKinsey, though largely unknown to the public, is an important name in the high and inner circles of government. We'd all like to tell the government what to do once in a while. Well, McKinsey not only tells government what to do, but the government listens and pays them for the advice.

Robert Fry of McKinsey talked to us.

ROONEY:

What would your contracts with government run to? A hundred thousand dollars? A hundred million dollars?

FRY (laughs):

Well, there was one with the Department of Transportation that we just finished, a study over there for Secretary Brinegar. That contract was quoted in Jack Anderson's column at three hundred and sixty-five thousand dollars— which I assume is about right.

ROONEY:

Would you, at the same time, be doing work for General Motors when you were doing something for the Department of Transportation?

FRY:

Oh, I think the sense of your question is, could we be serving an industrial client. And the answer is yes. But we would be serving it from a different office with different people. We have internal controls to make sure that there's no conflict.

ROONEY:

What about just a list of the government agencies that you do work for. Is that an available thing or is that a secret?

FRY:

Well, let me tell you some that I know have appeared in the press or otherwise been mentioned publicly over the last few years.

ROONEY:

In other words, there are some that you wouldn't . . .

FRY:

There are some I prefer . . .

ROONEY:

Prefer not to mention?

FRY:

Not to mention. We serve the Veterans Administration, the Peace Corps, the Department of Transportation that I mentioned earlier.

ROONEY:

But the ones that interest me most are the ones that you won't tell me.

FRY:

That's a representative list. We serve the Office of Management and Budget, the Treasury Department.

ROONEY:

Why wouldn't you tell me all of them?

FRY:

It's simply a practice of the firm that we're not the ones who tell publicly who our clients are.

ROONEY:

In other words, the government would come to you and give you this contract and say, ''But don't tell anybody about it.''

FRY:

No, they don't say that. I'm not trying to dodge your

question. I'm just being true to the standard practice of the
firm, which is a carry-over largely from the private sector.
But we still observe it here to the extent that our relationship with a client is not widely known.

ROONEY:

Is there a way we could find out what McKinsey's total
income for one year was from government contracts?

FRY:

Well, it would be in the several-hundred-thousand-dollar
range.

ROONEY:

Well, that one you mentioned was three hundred and
eighty-five thousand, so—

FRY:

Yes.

ROONEY:

It certainly would be several hundred.

FRY:

Yeah.

Power is always slipping away from most of us and into the
hands of the very few. I guess we all worry about it, but if
you spend some time in Washington, you get thinking that
Congress, at least, isn't really very dangerous. Democracy
still has the upper hand.

Almost everything we do is a fact before Congress knows
what's happened. Take sex, for instance, or the economy, if
sex offends you. Our national habits have changed in regard
to both sex and money, but Congress didn't have a thing to do
with either of them. We establish our own rules of how we
live and all Congress can do is make them official and make
them apply to everybody the same way.

Even if a congressman wanted to become some kind of a

dictator, he couldn't do it. He's too busy. Congress is disorganized, overworked, and very little of what it does becomes law. If one congressman is *for* something, another is against it. We're lucky they don't get along because if offers all of us a great deal of protection.

We can't get cameras into the House of Representatives gallery, so we don't have film of a little argument that we saw break out one day between Congressman James Cleveland of New Hampshire and Congressman Pierre duPont of Delaware. We went to their offices later and talked to each of them about that.

ROONEY:

I heard you speak on the floor of the House a few days ago. You were trying to get money for people in a ski area. They said they were in trouble because it hadn't snowed much. Is protecting businessmen from the elements a function of government?

CLEVELAND:

I think so. I'm sure you're acquainted with flood insurance and disaster insurance. And I think that we have various federal programs to assist people that have been victims of some natural disaster.

ROONEY:

Is not-snowing a natural disaster?

CLEVELAND:

Well, apparently, it didn't fall within the provisions of any existing law, and that's why I got the amendment through that I did.

DUPONT:

My reaction to that is we've come to the ultimate in government now. . . . We're paying people because it isn't snowing where they live.

ROONEY:

But what do you say to Congressman Cleveland, who says there are five thousand people in New Hampshire who aren't going to eat well enough because it didn't snow—they need help.

DUPONT:

Well, you say, "Jim Cleveland, you're a good friend and you're a nice guy, but we shouldn't be paying people because it doesn't snow. If it doesn't snow, it doesn't snow, and that's one of the things that we live with."

CLEVELAND:

The ski industry is really quite important to northern New England and northern New York. It employs a great many people and it particularly employs a lot of college students who are attending colleges in those areas. It's weekend work for them when most of the action is—

ROONEY:

But that day on the floor of the House, I was sort of amused and I suppose you weren't. Congressman duPont said that it had been raining in Rehoboth Beach, Delaware, where he has a lot of constituents, and the people who sold bikinis were in trouble there and he wondered if they would be eligible for support because it was raining at the beach.

CLEVELAND:

Well, the answer is that if there was a prolonged period of rain and dismal weather, I would think that a resort-type area might be eligible for this.

DUPONT:

Well, the other thing you can say to him, although he probably wouldn't like it is, "Jim, if we start the subsidies this year, and it snows less next year, you'll be back for more. It's an endless program. And furthermore, if it *does* snow next year, you'll be back for this amount anyhow, because you'll say if we stop the subsidies now nobody will make any money, and the result is pretty soon we'll be paying people whether it snows or not."

Congressmen and women do most of their work in committee session. A lot of those are closed to the public but a lot are open too. Tourists ought to spend more time at these and less time hanging around down by the Washington Monument.

We listened in on about thirty committees. You often pick up interesting bits of information.

MR. MAGNUSON:
   The price of wheat to the farmer is a very small item in the price of a loaf of bread whether it goes up or down.
CHAIRMAN:
   That's very true.
MR. MAGNUSON:
   And there are many occasions, I guess you've found out, where the price of wheat would go down and the price of a loaf of bread would go up.
CHAIRMAN:
   Could you, for the record, and the record will stay opened...

In Washington, everything is for the record . . . which usually means, let's not waste time with it.

Washington is probably the only place in the whole world where there are more writers than readers. Everyone is writing something, having it duplicated or printed and distributing it to everyone else. No one, it seems, is actually reading much of it.

The U.S. Government Printing Office in Washington has committed more words to more paper than any other printing plant in the whole world. The *Congressional Record* alone is a monumental job of printing. Eight hundred and thirty Linotype operators and editors work all night putting it out every day.

We counted a more or less average day's *Congressional Record*. There were four thousand more than half a million words in it. And that's just for one day.

Let me read you the way Congress opens each session. First there's a prayer, uniting church and state, and then the Speaker of the House or the Senate makes a motion; in this case it was Senator Mansfield. He says, "Mr. President, I ask unanimous consent that the readings of the *Journal* of the proceedings of [the previous day] be dispensed with."

Well, consent is always given. Thank God. Because it would take sixty solid hours to get through reading just this one day's *Congressional Record*. And by that time, of course, they could have had three more sessions of Congress and three more editions of the *Congressional Record*, each containing half a million words.

Words. Behind the fireproof doors at the Federal Records Center are two and a half million boxes of words that probably ought to be burned.

(Inside Federal Records Center) These cardboard coffins are headed for the crypt. They're being saved not so much because they're important but because, like your own Sunday paper, someone couldn't stand the thought of throwing them out without reading them . . . and they couldn't stand the thought of reading them.

Filing costs the government $2.8 billion a year, about thirteen dollars apiece for every American.

Your name is in here somewhere . . . and so is your father's.

The joke in government is that before you throw anything out, you Xerox it so you'll have a copy.

Not all government records are kept, though. The Pentagon is a regular secrets factory—and most of the secrets it produces every day are destroyed right where they're made. The Pentagon Disposal Center is the biggest secrets disposal mill in the whole universe. When people from a Pentagon office have papers they want to destroy, they bundle them up, bring them to the disposal center, sign for them and stand by until they have been chewed and digested by the paper shredder.

According to a usually reliable Pentagon source, there are, in addition to the secrets, usually a few unfinished crossword puzzles that go in there to be uncycled.

ROONEY:
About how much of this do you run through a day?
PAPER-SHREDDER SUPERVISOR:
Well, on the average of ten to fourteen tons of dry paper.
ROONEY:
And those are all *secrets?*
SUPERVISOR:
All secrets as far as I'm concerned.

ROONEY:

Boy, ten tons of secrets is a lot, isn't it?

SUPERVISOR:

Yep.

ROONEY:

Do you ever get curious about what's on those?

SUPERVISOR:

No, sir. You get to the point where you don't pay any attention to what goes in.

ROONEY:

And there's no possibility of anybody reading this, is there?

SUPERVISOR:

I'd say. Take a look at it. *(Picks up wet pulp)* If you can read that, why, I'll give you my next month's salary.

You might think the government isn't aware of the proliferation of paperwork in its operation. Wrong. The government has had studies done of the problem . . . lots of them.

"We've had a study done"; that's what you hear all over Washington. Having a study done is an end in itself. Actually *doing* something about a study is something else.

We went in to talk to Mark Koenig, who was called Assistant Archivist for Records Management. He was sort of in charge of trying to cut down on government paperwork.

ROONEY:

What's the cost of government paperwork?

KOENIG:

The last estimate we had from the General Accounting Office is fifteen billion dollars a year.

ROONEY:

Fifteen billion for paperwork.

The Paper Management Office tries to encourage people to cut down on paperwork by having a contest every year.

We have one of the letters sent out by a department head telling his people how to enter their nominees. It says: "The purpose of the award is to honor those Federal employees who have contributed significantly to the efficiency or cost reduction of Federal paperwork systems. Nominating procedures are described in the prospectus, but one change is necessary; six (6) copies of any nomination, rather than four (4), should be submitted."

Well, that's a bad start when you're trying to save paper.

The awards ceremony itself was a combination luncheon and cocktail party. It began at eleven-fifteen in the morning. It was a big event and very pleasant, but not in itself a good example of saving paper. There was paper everywhere you looked and in great quantity. You wonder whether maybe the paperwork award wasn't costing the government more in paper than it was saving it.

(Music, military march)

We weren't sure why the paperwork award ceremony was opened with a military color guard marching into the dining room . . . but, of course, we'd never been to a paper-saving award ceremony before, so what do we know?

This was the Super Bowl of paper-saving. We thought they were picking just one government money-saver, but it turns out there were lots of them. They gave out forty-one awards, some of them to as many as eight people. Actually, you could come away from this affair with the idea that the government wasn't *wasting* money at all on paper . . . that it was actually making money on it.

OFFICIAL GIVING AWARDS:
   . . . during the last nine years have been responsible for savings in excess of one billion dollars. . . .

Saving this kind of money, we could become a rich nation again.

(Applause)

VARIOUS VOICES:

"Congratulations."

"Thank you."

"You going to go and have a drink with us?"

"Say, that would be great."

"I'm not going back to the office."

"Oh, you're not?"

UNITED STATES GOVERNMENT

Memorandum

DEPARTMENT OF JUSTICE

Office of Management & Finance

TO : Heads of Offices, Divisions, and Boards of the Department of Justice

DATE: June 20, 1974

FROM : Jack Rottman
Chief, Personnel Section
Operations Support Staff

SUBJECT: Tenth Annual Federal Paperwork Management Awards
Response Due: July 23, 1974

The Washington Chapter of the Association of Records Executives and Administrators, in cooperation with the National Archives and Records Service of GSA, is currently accepting nominations for the Tenth Annual Federal Paperwork Management Awards.

As mentioned in the attached prospectus, the purpose of the award is to honor those Federal employees who have contributed significantly to the efficiency or cost reduction of Federal paperwork systems or programs.

Nominating procedures are described in the prospectus, but one change is necessary; six (6) copies of any nomination, rather than four (4), should be submitted to the Personnel Section, Main Building, Room 6229 by COB July 23, 1974.

If you have any questions, contact Mr. Warren Oser on extension 4615.

There's almost always someplace to go except back to work in Washington. There are a thousand little parties every week and it seems as though some people go to all of them.

In Washington, the amenities often take up more time than the business. The pace of the city is slower than in the cities that make something. There are more times out, more days off. "Lunch" doesn't always mean eating.

ROONEY:

You do this on your lunch hour?

1ST JOGGER:

Or, whenever.

ROONEY:

There's a lot of this going on in Washington. How come?

2ND JOGGER:

It just seems to be that way, I don't know.

ROONEY:

What's your job?

2ND JOGGER:

Over in the Pentagon.

ROONEY:

How many miles do you run a day?

3RD JOGGER:

Five.

ROONEY:

Five miles. Where do you work?

3RD JOGGER:

Pentagon.

Everything will still be here tomorrow. The government isn't *making* anything.

The United States government pays out something like $95 billion a year in subsidies. It seems as though every company and every professional organization has an office in Washington to represent its interests.

There's the National Soft Drink Association, the International Association of Fire Chiefs, the National Swimming Pool Institute, the Associated Telephone Answering Exchanges, the National Automobile Association, the Humane Society of the United States, the National Education Association, the National Rifle Association of America, the Society of American Foresters, the American Horse Council, the American Chemical Society, the Tobacco Institute. . . .

Almost every bill passed in Congress influences the distribution of money, and the game is to get more out of the government than you're putting in. A lot of people are winning the game.

Everyone knows the tax break the big oil companies get, but you don't hear much about the others. The lumber industry, for instance, gets a subsidy of $130 million. The federal government pays out $244 million to fourteen shipping companies. Every American seaman is subsidized for about $12,000. And that's in addition to what the shipping company pays the sailor.

And you don't have to look to the giants of industry either to find money being handed out. I was wandering through the Rayburn Congressional Office Building one day and came on an Association of Beekeepers trying to talk Congress out of some money.

MAN *(in cage with bees):*
But without the humble honeybee, agriculture couldn't survive. There's about ninety plants in agriculture—blueberries, apples, oranges, lemons, lots of other plants—where the honeybee is completely indispensable. We have to have the services of this little animal, again to bring the male and the female plants together.

ROONEY:
Are you a beekeeper?

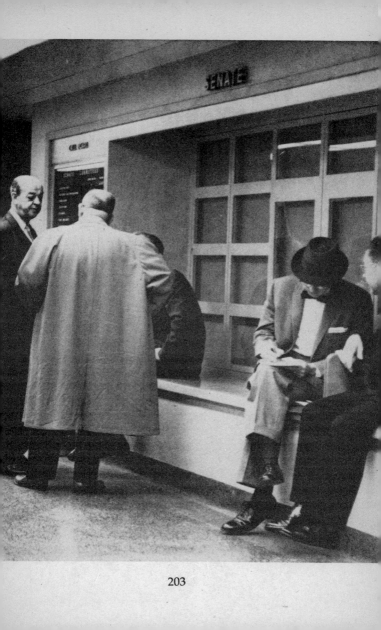

1ST MAN:

No. We're honey processors.

ROONEY:

I see. And what is the purpose of this meeting?

1ST MAN:

The purpose is to educate the Congress on the needs of the honey people.

ROONEY:

How much help from the government does the honey business get?

2ND MAN:

If you want me to be very candid, we don't get as much as we would like. We would like to get more help, that's one of the reasons we're up here today.

ROONEY:

What sort of help do you need from the government?

2ND MAN:

Well, for instance, insecticide poisoning sometimes kills our colonies, and, of course, that stops our production.

ROONEY:

Are you reimbursed for that?

2ND MAN:

We are reimbursed for this.

ROONEY:

Have you personally gotten money from the government?

2ND MAN:

Yes, I have. On a couple of different occasions, very small amounts.

ROONEY:

And how much did you get?

2ND MAN:

Ah . . .

ROONEY:

Roughly?

2ND MAN:
   Five hundred dollars.

Well, he isn't the only one who got a little something. It turns out that last year alone we paid a million and a half dollars to beekeepers who said some of their bees had died under unfortunate circumstances. It's all perfectly legal. You don't have to be dishonest to get rich off the government.

One of the reasons many of us don't feel so good about government is we've had dealings with the people who work in it. Ideals like democracy are only pure and clear in a book or at a distance where you can't make out any of the details. Good government doesn't seem nearly so good when you're being run around by some junior clerk in the license bureau.

But we're determined not to be all negative. There *are* good things about Washington and there *are* some very good public servants.

We talked to some people who *aren't* heads of departments, *don't* have any big deals going and *aren't* in the headlines. They're just competent people working in government jobs.

Phillip Hughes of the General Accounting Office is one of them. He and his wife came here from Seattle twenty-five years ago and still live in the same house they bought then. On the three mornings a week he plays handball, Mr. Hughes doesn't get in till almost eight o'clock.

ROONEY:
   Did you choose government as a career or did it just sort of happen to you?
HUGHES (*laughs*):
   I guess I'm not real sure. I think, at least periodically, I rechose it. I'm a product of the Depression era, as most of

us—all of us—my age are. And I was concerned when I was in college with the kinds of things that got us in the plight we were then in and about ways to get out of it.

That led me to get in the business of social and economic research and that got me into government. And I've been sort of plowing my way along ever since.

ROONEY:

Has there been any change in the attitude of people going into government?

HUGHES:

I think interest in government and the enthusiasm for it waxes and wanes depending on what's going on. I think the Kennedy and Johnson years brought a burst of interest on the part of young people in particular, and perhaps on everybody's part, in government—some feeling that government could save the world.

We've been disillusioned from that, those of us who were or who may have been at least partly convinced of it. But from my standpoint, I've found the government a continuing source of fascination. And an opportunity, at least at times, to feel that you have some grip on the world in which we live and on your own personal destiny and future.

ROONEY:

I'm interested in your saying that you're disillusioned. You mean from time to time you have been?

HUGHES:

Yes, I think we had more confidence in the sixties that good federal programs well administered could do things, could eliminate poverty, and so on. Those good programs won't do it by themselves.

ROONEY:

Is there too much government in America?

HUGHES:

Well, again, as a bureaucrat, that's a terrible question to ask me. But I guess I don't think so. There needs to be a central, at least a central source of inspiration, a source of exploration, and it seems to me government is really the only place to do that. But it needs to be done better than we've done it.

ROONEY:

In general terms, do you find the government represents the public interest or its own interest? Is it a self-perpetuating organization?

HUGHES:

Well, all organizations tend to perpetuate themselves . . . all organizations and individuals. That's the nature of the world. But I think government more nearly represents the public interest than any other entity that we have.

And I find it quite responsive. Most public servants, whether elected or appointed or bureaucratic, as I am in a sense, I think, want to respond to their perception of the public interest.

Now, nobody's perfect in perceiving it . . . but I think most of us in government try.

So that's some of what we found out about Washington.

Our society has become so interested in the visual aspects of everything it's easy to forget that there are no pictures of the most interesting things that go on in the world.

In Washington, it's not only hard to get pictures, it's hard to find out anything about *anything*. People hide things that there's no *reason* for them to hide.

Everyone has a public-relations person who is more interested in obscuring the truth than in revealing it. Every time you ask a question, they give you the impression they aren't thinking so much about what the *honest* answer is, but about what answer would make them *look* best. The truth doesn't enter into it unless it happens to coincide with their own best interests.

Now, that doesn't make government people unique, of course, but it makes you madder when you're being deceived with your own money.

It's very apparent that we all ought to know more about what's going on in Washington. The people who think *everything* is wrong down there are as far from the truth as the people who don't think *anything* is wrong.

It's not being run by evil people. It's being run by people like you and me.

And you know how we have to be watched.

Ourselves

D-DAY

If you're young and not really clear what D-Day was, let me tell you it was a day unlike any other.

There've only been a handful of days since the beginning of time on which the direction the world was taking has been changed in one twenty-four-hour period by an act of man. June 6, 1944, was one of them.

We all have days of our lives that stand out from the blur of days that have gone by. This is one of mine, if I may impose it on you.

I landed on the beaches of France four days after D-Day thirty-five years ago. No one can tell the whole story of D-Day. Each of the 60,000 men who waded ashore that day knew a little part of the story too well. To them the landing looked like a catastrophe. Each knew a friend shot through the throat, shot through the knee. Each knew the first names of five hanging dead on the barbed wire offshore, three who

lay unattended on the beach as the blood drained from the holes in their bodies. They knew whole tank crews drowned when the tanks were unloaded in twenty feet of water.

There were heroes here no one will ever know because they're dead. The heroism of others is known only to themselves.

Across the Channel in England, the war directors were remote from the details of tragedy. They saw no blood. From the statisticians' distant view, the invasion looked like a great success. They were right. We're always defeated by statisticians, even in victory.

What the Americans and the British and the Canadians— don't forget the Canadians—were trying to do was get back a whole continent that had been taken from its rightful owners. It was one of the most monumentally unselfish things one group of people ever did for another.

It's hard for anyone who's been in a war to describe the terror of it to anyone who hasn't.

"Here," the battleground guide says when the tourists come, "they fought the bloody battle for the beach." He talks on with a pointer in his hand to a busload of people about events that never happened, in a place they never were.

How would anyone know that John Lacey died in that clump of weeds by the wagon path as he looked to his left toward Simpson and caught a bullet behind the ear? And if there had been a picture of it—and there weren't any—it wouldn't have shown that Lacey was the only one who carried apples for the guys in his raincoat pocket.

If you think the world is rotten, go to the cemetery at Saint-Laurent-sur-Mer on the hill overlooking the beach. See what one group of men did for another, D-Day, June 6, 1944.

AN ESSAY ON WAR

We are all inclined to believe that our generation is more civilized than the generations that preceded ours.

From time to time, there is even some substantial evidence that we hold in higher regard such civilized attributes as compassion, pity, remorse, intelligence and a respect for the customs of people different from ourselves.

Why war then?

Some pessimistic historians think the whole society of man runs in cycles and that one of the phases is war.

The optimists, on the other hand, think war is not like an eclipse or a flood or a spell of bad weather. They believe that it is more like a disease for which a cure could be found if the cause were known.

Because war is the ultimate drama of life and death, stories and pictures of it are more interesting than those about peace. This is so true that all of us, and perhaps those of us in

television more than most, are often caught up in the action of war to the exclusion of the ideas of it.

If it is true, as we would like to think it is, that our age is more civilized than ages past, we must all agree that it's very strange that in the twentieth century, our century, we have killed more than 70 million of our fellowmen on purpose, at war.

It is very, very strange that since 1900 more men have killed more other men than in any other seventy years in history.

Probably the reason we are able to do both—that is, believe on one hand that we *are* more civilized and on the other hand wage war to kill—is that killing is not so personal an affair in war as it once was. The enemy is invisible. One man doesn't look another in the eye and run him through with a sword. The enemy, dead or alive, is largely unseen. He is killed by remote control: a loud noise, a distant puff of smoke and then . . . silence.

The pictures of the victim's wife and children, which he carries in his breast pocket, are destroyed with him. He is not heard to cry out. The question of compassion or pity or remorse does not enter into it. The enemy is not a man, he is a statistic. It is true, too, that more people are being killed at war now than previously because we're better at doing it than we used to be. One man with one modern weapon can kill thousands.

The world's record for killing was set on August 6, 1945, at Hiroshima.

There have been times in history when one tribe attacked another for no good reason except to take its land or its goods, or simply to prove its superiority. But wars are no longer fought without some ethical pretension. People want to believe they're on God's side and he on theirs. One nation does not usually attack another anymore without first having propagandized itself into believing that its motives are honorable. The Japanese didn't attack Pearl Harbor with any sense in their own minds that they were scheming, deceitful or infamous.

Soldiers often look for help to their religion. It was in a frenzy of religious fervor that Japanese Kamikaze pilots died in World War II with eternal glory on their minds. Even a just God, though, listening to victory prayers from both sides, would be understandably confused.

It has always seemed wrong to the people who disapprove of war that we have spent much of our time and half of our money on anti-creation. The military budget of any major power consumes half of everything and leaves us half to live on.

It's interesting that the effective weapons of war aren't developed by warriors, but by engineers. In World War I they made a machine that would throw five hundred pounds of steel fifty miles. They compounded an ingeniously compressed package of liquid fire that would burn people like bugs. The engineers are not concerned with death, though.

The scientist who splits an atom and revolutionizes warfare isn't concerned with warfare; his mind is on that fleck of matter.

And so we have a machine gun a man can carry that will spit out two hundred bullets a minute, each capable of ripping a man in two, although the man who invented it, in all probability, loves his wife, children, dogs, and probably wouldn't kill a butterfly.

Plato said that there never was a good war or a bad peace, and there have always been people who believed this was true. The trouble with the theory is that the absence of war isn't necessarily peace. Maybe the worst thing Adolf Hitler did was to provide evidence for generations to come that any peace is *not* better than any war. Buchenwald wasn't war.

The generation that had found Adolf Hitler hard to believe, was embarrassed at how reluctant it had been to go help the people of the world who needed help so desperately. That generation determined not to be slow with help again and as a result may have been too quick. A younger generation doesn't understand why the United States went into Vietnam. Having gotten into the war, all it wanted to consider itself a winner was to get out. Unable to make things the way it wanted them, but unwilling to accept defeat, it merely changed what is wanted.

DWIGHT EISENHOWER, 1962: "I think it's only defense, self-defense, that's all it is."

JOHN KENNEDY, 1963: "In the final analysis it's their war. They're the ones that have to win it or lose it."

LYNDON JOHNSON, 1969: "But America has not changed her essential position. And that purpose is peaceful settlement."

RICHARD NIXON, 1974: "But the time has come to end this war."

There are a lot of reasons for the confusion about a war. One of them is that the statesmen who make the decisions never have to fight one themselves. Even the generals don't fight the battles.

Professional soldiers often say they hate war, but they would be less than human if they did not, just once, want to play the game they spent a lifetime practicing. How could you go to West Point for four years and not be curious about whether you'd be any good in a war?

Even in peacetime, nations keep huge armies. The trouble with any peacetime all-volunteer army is that the enlisted men in one are often no smarter than the officers. During a war when the general population takes up arms, the character of an army changes and for the better.

In the twentieth century there is open rebellion between the

people who decide about whether to fight or not and some of the young men being asked to do the fighting. It hasn't always been that way. Through the years, even the reluctant draftees have usually gone to battle with some enthusiasm for it. Partially the enthusiasm comes from the natural drama of war and the excitement of leaving home on a crusade. It's a trip to somewhere else, and with the excitement inherent in an uncertain return. It is a great adventure, with the possibility of being killed the one drawback to an otherwise exciting time in life.

There have been just and unjust wars throughout history

but there is very little difference in the manner in which people have been propagandized to believe in them. Patriotism, sometimes no more knowing or sophisticated than pride in a high-school football team, is the strongest motivator. With flags enough and martial music enough, anyone's blood begins to boil.

Patriotic has always been considered one of the good things to be in any nation on earth, but it's a question whether patriotism has been a force for good or evil in the world.

Once the young men of a country get into a battle, most of them are neither heroes nor cowards. They're swept up in a movement that includes them and they go where they're told to go, do what they're told to do. It isn't long before they're tired and afraid and they want to go home.

True bravery is always highly regarded because we recognize that someone has done something that is good for all of us, certainly at the risk and possibly at the expense of his own life. But in war, the mantle of virtue is pressed on every soldier's head as though they were all heroes. This is partly because everyone else is grateful to him and wants to encourage him to keep at it. All soldiers who come home alive are heaped with the praise that belongs to very few of them . . . and often to the dead they left behind.

In part, at least, this accounts for why so many men like being ex-soldiers. Once the war and the fighting are done with and they are safe at home, it matters not that they may have served in the 110th emergency shoe-repair battalion. In their own eyes, they are heroes of the front lines.

Even in retrospect, though, a nation has always felt an obligation to honor its warriors. The face of the earth is covered with statuary designed for this purpose which is so bad in many cases that were it not in honor of the dead, it would evoke not tears but laughter.

During and since World War II, the United States alone has bestowed ten million medals and ribbons of honor on its soldiers, many of them for acts calling for as little courage as living a year in Paris.

Bravery is as rare in war as it is in peace. It isn't just a matter of facing danger from which you would prefer to run. If a man faces danger because the alternative to doing that is worse or because he doesn't understand the danger, this may make him a good soldier but it is something other than bravery. Stupidity faces danger easier than intelligence.

The average bright young man who is drafted hates the whole business because an army always tries to eliminate the individual differences in men. The theory is that a uniformity of action is necessary to achieve a common goal. That's good for an army but terrible for an individual who likes himself the way he is.

Some men, of course, like the order imposed on them. They like the freedom from making hard decisions that mindless submission to authority gives them.

There is always more precision on the drill field back home than there is on the battlefield. Uniformity of action becomes less precise as an army approaches the front. At the front it usually disappears altogether. It is not always, or even usually, the best marchers who make the best fighters.

Everyone talks as though there was nothing good about war, but there are some good things and it's easy to see why so many people are attracted by it. If there were no good things about war, the chances are we would find a way not to have another.

A nation at war feels a unity it senses at no other time. Even the people not fighting are bound together. There is a sense of common cause missing in peacetime. Accomplishments are greater, change is quicker . . . and if progress is motion, there is more of it in wartime. A nation at peace is

busy gratifying itself, overeating, overdressing, lying in the sun until it's time to eat and drink again.

If war brings out the worst in people as it has been assumed it does, it also brings out the very best. It's the ultimate competition. Most of us live our lives at half speed, using only as much of our ability as is absolutely necessary to make out. But at war if a man is actually fighting it, he uses all his brain and all his muscle. He explores depths of his emotions he didn't know were down there and might never have occasion to use again in his lifetime. He lives at full speed, finding strength he didn't know he had accomplishing things he didn't know he could do.

The best thing about war is hard to describe, is never talked about. Most of us get a warm sense of fellow feeling when we act in close and successful relationship with others, and maybe that happens more in war than any other time. There is a lonesomeness about life that no one who has experienced it likes to talk about, and acting together for a common cause, men often come closest to what they ought to be at their very best.

It is paradoxical but true that in war when man is closest to death, he is also closest to complete fulfillment and farthest from loneliness. He is dependent, dependable, loved and loving.

And there is another thing about war. If there is love in us, there is hate too and it's apparent that hate springs from the same well as love and just as quickly. No one is proud of it but hate is not an unpleasant emotion and there is no time other than wartime when we are encouraged to indulge ourselves in an orgy of hate.

The worst of war is hell but there isn't much of the worst of it and not many soldiers experience even that much.

A soldier at war doesn't feel the need to answer any questions about it. He is exhausted by the battle.

He is busy destroying and it does not occur to him that he will have to help rebuild the world he is pulling down.

He often mistakes the exultation of victory for a taste of what things will be like for the rest of his life.

And they are only like that for a very short time.

YOUTH

The other night on television someone was interviewing a former football player named Andy Robustelli. Andy said he thought there were more injuries in the game today because the young men playing weren't made of the same stuff they were when he played.

It reminded me that about the time Robustelli played I heard President Eisenhower, speaking in Abilene, Kansas, say that moral standards weren't as high among the youth as they were when he was planting sweet corn in his backyard there.

For as far back as I can remember, people have been saying the youth of the nation is getting soft and losing its moral fiber. I just doubt it. They certainly aren't wearing as much underwear but I doubt if there's any less moral fiber. I'll bet the very day Andy Robustelli put on his first jockstrap, some old athlete was saying athletes weren't what they used to be.

I'll bet the day little Ike Eisenhower was planting that sweet corn, someone was saying kids wouldn't work anymore.

Last Thanksgiving some clergyman in Chicago was complaining about sexual freedom among the young. He said he wondered what the Pilgrims would think if they could see the dances the kids are doing today instead of the minuet.

Frankly, I think the pioneers would watch for a few minutes and then try to get with it. We are all evidence of the fact that the Pilgrim Fathers weren't always minueting. For every Pilgrim Father there was a Pilgrim Mother.

I think the reason for all these disparaging remarks by the old about the young is obvious. Because of the intimations of death in the color of their hair, the stoop of their shoulder or the sag of their chin, older people are at a disadvantage with the young and they know it.

Elders resent the suggestion, implicit in young people's attitude, that they are young as a matter of their own choice. As a result, older people try to get even by saying kids aren't what *they* used to be when they were kids.

It's just amazing how long this country has been going to hell without ever having got there.

HAIR

Next to death, commercial bread and the price of gas, I hate the idea of getting bald the most. I'm not really *getting* very bald yet and I'm pleased about that, but when I do, I'm not going to try and hide it. All anyone who's getting bald looks like when they try to hide it is like someone getting bald trying to hide it.

Some men let what little they have grow long and then spread it around. If someone wears a toupee—it looks like either a good toupee or a bad toupee, but it usually looks like a toupee. In the best toupee shops in the country, a good hairpiece costs about eight hundred dollars. Of course, over the long run, you make it up in haircuts.

I don't know *why* we're so sensitive about getting bald. A lot of men look good bald. They often look distinguished and important. Some men are even bald on purpose. It can even be a trademark.

Often the amount of hair on a man's head is sort of a political statement. You can tell a Reagan supporter from a Kennedy man.

One of the great mysteries of life is why some men have such an easy time growing hair on their face . . . and a hard time growing it on their head. You can't talk to a man about how he likes his hair. On the tennis court, Jimmy Connors looks terrible with long, stringy, wet hair. I suppose he likes the way it looks when he isn't playing tennis, although it doesn't look all that good then, either.

I'm very suspicious of a man who fusses much with his hair. It can be there or not be there, but he ought not to spend half his life arranging it. He ought to comb it once in the morning and maybe once in the middle of the day if he gets caught in the wind. Otherwise a man ought to leave his hair alone.

(To camera) Okay, cut. How was that? All right? How did—did I look all right on that? Let's—let's take it again.

EYEGLASSES

Do you wear glasses—yet, I mean? Because if you don't, you will. I never thought I would, but I do, for reading and writing.

I think most people fight wearing glasses and they ought to. We all have some obligation not to give in easily to deterioration of any kind.

It's a funny thing that even though most of us don't like the idea of wearing glasses because we don't think we look as good with them on, we don't think anyone *else* looks any *worse* wearing them. As a matter of fact, we all have friends who'd look strange if they *didn't* have their glasses on. They look like themselves with them; they'd look funny without them.

When I first got glasses, the doctor told me they wouldn't weaken my eyes. I mean, he said they wouldn't make me dependent on them. I don't think he knew what he was talking about. My eyes certainly got worse within a year after I started wearing glasses. I *was* dependent on them. Of course, I was a year older, too, so how are you going to know for sure which did it?

I got thinking about glasses because of an awful thing that happened to me two weeks ago. I was going out to dinner Saturday night, so I shaved twice that day. I was shaving away and feeling my face for whiskers, the way a man does, and sure enough I felt some. I *felt* them, but I couldn't *see* them.

I put my glasses on and, by golly, there they were—whiskers.

And that was the terrible thing that happened. I realized then that I need my glasses to shave with and I'm going to have to reorganize my whole system of getting up in the morning so I have glasses with me in the bathroom.

There are certain ways we all judge our own age other than by our birthdays, and I feel older now.

TYPES

There are only two types of people in the world, Type A and Type Z. It isn't hard to tell which type you are. How long before the plane leaves do you arrive at the airport?

Early plane catchers, Type A, pack their bags at least a day in advance, and they pack neatly. If they're booked on a flight that leaves at four in the afternoon, they get up at five-thirty that morning. If they haven't left the house by noon, they're worried about missing the plane.

Late plane catchers, Type Z, pack hastily at the last minute and arrive at the airport too late to buy a newspaper.

What do you do with a new book? Type A reads more carefully and finishes every book, even though it isn't any good.

Type Z skims through a lot of books and is more apt to write in the margins with a pencil.

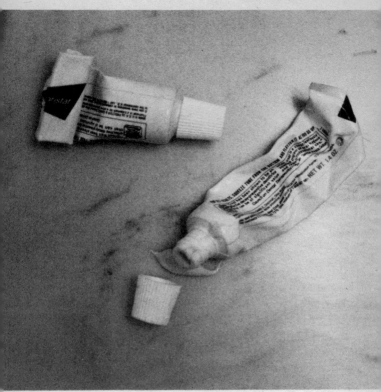

Type A eats a good breakfast; Type Z grabs a cup of coffee.

Type A's turn off the lights when leaving a room and lock the doors when leaving a house. They go back to make sure they've locked it, and they worry later about whether they left the iron on or not. They didn't.

Type Z's leave the lights burning and, if they lock the door at all when they leave the house, they're apt to have forgotten their keys.

Type A sees the dentist twice a year, has an annual physical checkup and thinks he may have something.

Type Z has been meaning to see a doctor.

Type A squeezes a tube of toothpaste from the bottom and rolls it very carefully as he uses it, puts the top back on every time.

Type Z squeezes the tube from the middle, and he's lost the cap under the radiator.

Type Z's are more apt to have some Type A characteristics than Type A's are apt to have any Type Z characteristics.

Type A's always marry Type Z's.
Type Z's always marry Type A's.

SAVERS

January is the time of year we're all faced with a difficult decision. What do you do with the Christmas cards?

Some of them are too beautiful to throw out . . . others have names and addresses on them you want to keep. On the other hand, most of us are up to here in junk at this time of year and something has to go.

I'm a saver myself. I save everything. I don't think I've ever thrown away a pair of shoes, for example. I have shoes in my closet that hurt so much or look so terrible I'll never wear them again . . . but there they are.

I'm hooked on old peanut-butter jars, too. We don't eat much peanut butter in my house but I make up for that by saving old mayonnaise and jam jars, too.

Coffee cans. How can you throw out such a nice clean can with this tight-fitting plastic top? Who knows when I'll need how many for cleaning paintbrushes in turpentine? These are

239

all from coffee we've made here in the office. I save them
here, too, even though I don't have to paint my own office.

Sometimes I like the boxes things come in better than
anything that comes in them. I keep old wine bottles, too. We
don't drink any more wine than we eat peanut butter, but I
keep the bottles on the shelf in the garage.

Up in the attic there are about six boxes and two big trunks
with the really good stuff I've saved. I have things like the
kids' old schoolwork papers, programs from school plays
with their names buried somewhere down near the bottom
with the angels . . . that kind of stuff.

There are two kinds of savers. The first is the practical saver who keeps string, bags and old aluminum foil as a practical matter. And then there's the sentimental saver. The sentimental savers can't stand the idea of throwing out any memory of their lives.

Unfortunately, I'm both kinds.

TELEPHONES

I like the telephone. It's a great invention. But there are a couple of problems with it. One problem is a lot of people like the telephone so much they use it even when they don't have anything to say.

One of my least favorite calls is from the person who dials my number, I pick up the phone and he says: "Hello, who's this?"

Who does he think it is—the Queen of England?

Most of us develop mannerisms on the phone—you know, with the instrument itself. For example, some people look off into the distance when they're on the telephone—big thinkers.

Other people seem to be trying to look over the wire so they can see the person they're talking to on the other end. They're very intense.

There are other telephoners who can't talk on the telephone unless they have a pad and a pencil in front of them. They do circles or squares or push-pulls. They doodle a lot.

I know several people around here who like to put their feet up on the desk when they talk on the telephone. They get so comfortable they hate to put their feet down.

There are certain people who have a knack for staying on the phone for hours without ever saying anything themselves. You know the type?

"Not really. Uh-huh. No, no. Yeah. Yeah. Yes. Yeah. Uh-huh . . . Who is this?"

Nervous executives like to stand when they talk. They often pace a lot. They have a long cord so they can move around. I think it gives them a feeling they're getting someplace in life.

And there are the cord-twisters. I hate to be the next one to use the telephone after a cord-twister's had it.

A lot of people can talk on the phone lying down. I can't do that. I have to at least get up on one elbow.

I don't know why the phone company has never come up with anything to solve the problem of how to talk on the phone when you're using both hands to do something else. A few newspaper reporters I've known were very good no-hands, usually with a cigarette in their mouth.

The person I really hate to get a call from is the semi-important executive who's too busy to make the call himself. You know how it goes: "Linda, get me Andy Rooney!"

I answer, and Linda says: "Please hold for Mr. Paley."

And there I am waiting for some guy I didn't want to talk to in the first place.

GENDER

Our President won't face any more serious issue while he's in office than the crisis that exists with the English language.

A lot of women think they're getting a dirty deal when it comes to English usage and they insist that some changes be made. One trouble, of course, is that Americans don't go by any set rules of grammar. We're inconsistent about how we use words to indicate whether the person is a man or a woman.

We call men actors "actors." We call woman actors "actresses."

On the other hand, we call men authors "authors"... women authors "authors."

Men waiters are "waiters." Women waiters are "waitresses."

Some of these problems just go away, of course. Years ago everyone called Amelia Earhart an "aviatrix." Well, you don't hardly see any aviatrixes anymore, or aviators either, for that matter. They're all just pilots now.

Some women insist we substitute "person" for "man" as a suffix on words. Recently a woman on Long Island went so far as to have her name officially changed from Goodman to Goodperson. Well, I'm not going to say whether I think that was right or wrong. I have absolutely no opinion about that kind of idiocy, but I don't think substituting "person" for "man" is the answer.

All of us want to do the right thing, but look what happens at a meeting when the chairman is a woman, for instance. There's always a confusion about what to call her.

WALTER CRONKITE:
　　... Audrey Rowe Colom of Washington, D.C., who is the Chairperson of the National Women's Political Caucus...
BARRY GOLDWATER, JR.:
　　Madame Chairman...
FEMALE VOICE:
　　... Chairwoman of the National Women's Political Caucus.
NELSON ROCKEFELLER:
　　And to Madame Chairman...

For a writer, the worst problem is what to use for the third person singular pronoun when you don't know whether the person is a man or a woman.

For instance, "Someone left *his* pen on my desk." Feminists resent the assumption it was a man, but it's too clumsy to say "Someone left *his or her* pen on my desk" every time.

What a lot of people do is avoid the problem by making an intentional grammatical error. They say, "Someone left *their* pen on my desk." Well, it was obviously only one person who left the pen but it bothers us less to make it plural than it does to offend women by using the universal "his."

Before the women's rights movement no one worried about it. "Man" in a general sense always meant women too.

246

"Man the lifeboats" didn't mean women weren't welcome on board.

On the other hand, there were always certain inanimate objects we made feminine. A sailboat, for instance . . . "*She's* a beauty!" The lift-off of a rocket . . . "There *she* goes!" A train coming around the bend . . . "Here *she* comes!"

Strangely enough, even though we call a sailboat "she," we always say, "She had a four-man crew," even when two of the crew are women. It's really a mess and it has to be cleared up. One suggestion has been to reverse things for a while. Men would get the sailboats, the rockets and the trains coming round the bend. Women could have manpower, manhole covers, manslaughter. . . . As a matter of fact, as far as I'm concerned, if it would make them happy, they can have all of mankind.

DIRTY WORDS

I'd like to talk about dirty words.

There are about 490,000 words in the English language, and the Supreme Court says there are only seven of them we can't use on television because they're obscene. This comes to mind now because of the showing of *Gone With the Wind* on television.

When that picture was first made, it wasn't shown in some cities because at the end of the picture Clark Gable says the word "damn," a profanity.

"Frankly, my dear, I don't give a damn!" he said.

Now, of course, there aren't any words they don't use in the movies. It seems to me we're awfully confused over how we feel about obscenities. We don't use them on television, good newspapers don't print them and yet movies and widely read books and magazines use all of them.

I'm not confused about how I feel. I don't like obscenities

and I don't use them. I don't even like to hear other people use them. This doesn't make me a wonderful person. We all decide which virtues to hold to and which to ignore. Not swearing's a minor virtue, but it's mine and I like myself for it. It's really more a matter of good and bad manners than anything else.

Why should anyone impose words on our ears that we don't want to hear, any more than they should throw food at our dining-room table?

I think a lot of dumb people do it because they can't think of what they want to say and they're frustrated. A lot of smart people do it to pretend they aren't very smart—want to be just one of the boys.

Women have been using more dirty words than they used to. I guess it gives them a feeling of being liberated. They want to be just one of the boys too.

Most people who use a lot of dirty words, or a few dirty words frequently, do it as a matter of habit. The words don't have any meaning to them when they say them.

There's certainly a place for obscenity and profanity in literature or any of the arts. When a novel's a mirror showing us to ourselves, it has to include some obscene things to make it true. But when writers start using more of it than people really use, that's not art; it's show business.

Not very funny tonight. Sorry.

MONEY

Every once in a while I wonder what in the world I've done with all the money I've made. Do you ever wonder that?

I began buying things with my own money in 1945, just after I was discharged from the Army. The other day I started making a list. This is very rough, but here it is.

Food for a family of six for 20 years, at two dollars a day per person, comes to $87,600. The kids have left home now, but my mother lives with us; that's three people for 15 years, at three dollars a day per person—food costs more now—comes to $49,275.

That's a total for food of $136,875.

It's hard to remember how many cars you've bought. I think I've bought 18 cars in 35 years for an average of maybe $3,500 a car. That's a total of $63,000 I've spent on cars.

We drive a total of about 50,000 miles a year. We have two cars. Gas costs $1.30 a gallon now, but it used to only cost 28 cents, so say an average of 35 cents a gallon. We get maybe 18 miles on a gallon of gas. So that's about 97,000 gallons of gas, at 35 cents a gallon, for a total of $34,000 we've spent on gas.

We bought the house in 1951 for twenty-nine five and, with a 20-year mortgage, the bank collected about $50,000 from me.

We put four kids through college, four years each at $6,000 a year apiece. That comes to a total of $96,000 for college. Sometimes I think we should have sent them to cheaper colleges and bought more expensive cars.

Heat, light, telephone, real-estate taxes, utilities in general, must have averaged $2,500 for 35 years. That's a total of $87,500.

Then there was miscellaneous: clothes, haircuts, crab-grass killer, sunglasses (I lose a lot of sunglasses), bourbon, beer, shoelaces, appliances, television sets. Say, $200,000 for miscellaneous.

Now I'm going to level with you. I've made a lot of money. You know, not a fortune, but more than most people. In 35 years, I suppose I made $1.25 million.

In addition to all these items, I guess I've paid about $400,000 in taxes. So, that's a grand total that I've spent of $1,067,375.

Now, tell me this. If I've made a million and a quarter and I've spent $1,067,000 . . . what the heck did I do with that other $183,000?

CALENDARS

There are half a dozen things that are basic to our lives that don't make any sense at all. They're basic and they're important, and why we don't change them I can't understand.

Take our calendar, for instance.

This is the beginning of the new year, right? Will someone please tell me how January 1st got to be the beginning of the year when we all know perfectly well it's right in the *middle* of the year?

The year actually ends just before the Fourth of July and it actually begins the day after Labor Day.

Here, look at this calendar for next year. Thanksgiving will be November 22nd . . . then a month and three days later we get Christmas . . . a week after that, New Year's.

We don't *need* three holidays that soon. When we need a holiday is in February, when everyone is sick and tired of winter.

Christmas obviously should be moved. No one knows for certain which day Christ was born on. And he certainly wouldn't mind if we celebrated Christmas in February. We could still make a week out of it without having New Year's Eve at the end of it. No one wants to go back to work again right after New Year's Eve.

If we moved Christmas to mid-February, that would make a lot more sense out of Thanksgiving. It's fun to get the whole family together for a turkey dinner at Thanksgiving . . . but not if it's just a month before the family gets together again for another turkey dinner at Christmas. There's just so much family or so much turkey anyone can take.

Now . . . about our summer vacation. Most of us take it in July or August—another thing that doesn't make sense. August is a nice name for a month but the weather isn't that good and the days are already getting shorter.

Here's the longest day of the year, June 21st. We should be on vacation while the days are almost at their longest but still getting longer. No one likes the feeling the days are getting shorter. It reminds us of our own mortality and that's nothing to be reminded of on vacation. *June* should be the principal vacation month.

So here's what I'm suggesting. Move the whole month of January, including my birthday, so that it falls between August and September.

Eliminate Labor Day altogether. Big Business doesn't have a day of its own and I don't think labor needs one. Under this new system, what was Labor Day will now be January 1st, New Year's Day.

There's still work to be done on days of the week too . . . but some other time.

VACATIONS

January is the time of year a lot of people start thinking about their vacations. The one they took last summer is almost paid for and their thoughts are turning to where they're going to go this time.

It strikes me that the idea we have to *go* somewhere on vacation has gotten out of hand. The first day back at work, everyone wants to know "Where'd you go on your vacation?"

You're supposed to say, "The south of France" or "We went to the seashore," "We went to the mountains," "We took a raft trip down the Colorado."

The trip isn't good enough unless you can't afford it.

Why do we always have to take off? I mean, let's face it, going somewhere is never easy. It's not always any fun, either. Getting there is a pain in the neck and coming back is even worse. For one thing, your clothes don't fit in the suitcase anymore.

I don't know where we got the idea we have to go away for a vacation. I suppose the travel industry sold it to us. The travel business is the second largest industry in the United States. It's always trying to get us to go someplace *else* to spend our money when most of us don't have any trouble spending it right where we are. The industry tries to make us all feel cheap if we don't go on an expensive trip.

Well, I've got my plans all made for my vacation. I'm not going *anywhere!* How do you like that, travel industry? Show me all the luxurious accommodations you want, tempt me with pictures of bikini-clad girls with windswept hair on pearl-white beaches—I'm not going. I'm staying put is what I'm doing. We've all been tourists, and none of us likes being a tourist, so this summer I'll be somewhere I've never been on vacation—right where I live.

I know what I'm going to do, too. All year long I worry because I don't have the time to do all those little jobs around the house. Well, for my three weeks' vacation next year I'm going to stay home. I'm not going to do those little jobs then, either.

For vacation, I'm just not going to worry about them.

MR. ROONEY GOES TO WORK*

(Police officer pulls Rooney to the side of the road.)
COP:

 Hi!
ROONEY:

 Hi, there.
COP:

 Can I see your driver's license, please?
ROONEY:

 Yep. We're doing a little story on working in America.
COP:

 I see.
ROONEY:

 Are policemen working as hard as they used to?
COP:

 Well, I don't know. . . .

---

* Broadcast July 5, 1977.

One cop in Janesville, Wisconsin, convinced us that he, at least, was working harder than was absolutely necessary.

When a writer sets out to report on something, he shouldn't have much of any idea in advance about what he's going to find out. That's nonsense, because of *course* he has some idea. The next best thing he can do is not let his preconceived ideas get in the way of what he actually *does* find out.

Last year some of us here at CBS thought we ought to do a report on "Work in America." It didn't seem as though anyone was working very hard and we were thinking of calling it "Goofing Off in America."

You know the story: everyone's leaning on his shovel; you can't get a plumber; they close at four o'clock; you have to make an appointment to have your car repaired two weeks before it breaks down; you read stories about strikes everywhere. . . . So I didn't go into this without an opinion.

To find out whether we were right or wrong, I set out across the country to talk to people and film them at work. I watched thousands of workers who didn't know I was watching. I talked to hundreds of them about their work. I talked to their employers and to their union leaders. In a few places they were reluctant to talk to me. For the most part, though, workers talked freely. They didn't seem afraid to say what they thought, even when the boss was standing there listening.

What follows is what one reporter found out about work in America.

The daily absentee rate in factories in the United States is about 5 percent. In other words, one out of every twenty workers is apt to be off the job any given day. On a nice summer Monday or Friday in Detroit, 15 percent of the workers are often officially "sick."

One out of every six Americans works for the federal, state or local government now. And there's general agreement, I think, that a government job brings out the *least* in people.

With vacations, three-day holidays, family emergencies and sick days, it seems as though a lot of us have as many days off as on now. Some of the new union contracts are calling for a work week so short they could make weekends obsolete.

So it's no wonder that there's a widespread opinion among Americans that Americans aren't working very hard.

WOMAN:
Well, I don't think that people do work hard . . . what they should work to get the money that they get.

ROONEY:
It's interesting that you would say that. I mean, you are in what would be called a blue-collar job, even though you

have a white turtleneck sweater on. But do you think the young people are not working as hard as they used to?

WOMAN:

I don't think anyone is.

SUPERINTENDENT:

Some of 'em have a "don't care" attitude. They just come and go. And years ago, why, everyone took pride in their work and of course they needed the money too. People have changed. That's for sure.

ROONEY:

Do you think young people are working hard? Other people your age? Are they working as hard as, say, your family did, or your grandparents?

COCKTAIL WAITRESS:

No, I don't think so.

ROONEY:

Given a thousand Japanese workers and a thousand American workers with the same tools, which group would produce the most?

TAIZO MATSUKAGI:

Ah, generally speaking, I would say probably Japanese.

FARMER:

I don't like to buy foreign material, but the Americans aren't doing so good on some of their stuff they put out. It isn't as good as it used to be. Too shiftless. I mean, they don't care. Years back, with the old machinery, the fellows that were building it took pride in what they were doing and they liked to have a good product when they got done. But now they're shoving it too fast.

ROONEY:

Do you think that's something in the American character or is it just this desire to make money on the part of the big companies?

FARMER:

Well, I can't answer all them questions . . . 'cause I don't really know.

ROONEY (*on Fort Lauderdale beach*):

People working as hard as they used to?

MARCEL MULBERRY:

Not in my book. We're in the apple business way up in the Champlain Valley, northern New York, and we have to get imported help from the Bahamas now to help us harvest the crop.

ROONEY:

People just won't work?

MULBERRY:

Well, they just don't care to work anymore. The local people, they'll come out a few hours and go home and be satisfied with fifteen dollars. They just don't like the hard work. That's all. They don't want to stay with it.

I read somewhere a statement made by a man named Sanford Noll, Chairman of the Curtis-Noll Corporation. He said that the trouble with the American worker is that he's making so much money, he takes off on vacation whenever he feels like it. Well, that was sort of a catchy remark, so we called Sanford Noll's office in Cleveland to see if we could come there and talk to him.

His secretary told us he'd taken off for Fort Lauderdale and wouldn't be back for six weeks. So we went to Fort Lauderdale to find him.

SANFORD NOLL:

A certain group of people make enough money and that's all they want. They're not looking to accumulate anything. They just want to work to make enough to get the things that they want out of life. And when they get a lot more, then a lot of these people work less.

I think the younger workers are a result of a very affluent society in which we live. . . . Their parents, who made very nominal incomes twenty, twenty-five years ago, make very good money now and they give their children the things they want so that the motivation, the incentive, I think, has been curtailed.

ROONEY:

Then how do you go about motivating them?

NOLL:

Through a relationship with their supervisor, company

newspapers, informing them as to what's going on. In that company newspaper, everyone's birthday, everyone's anniversary is printed. And through service awards.

ROONEY:

That's pretty sad as compared with giving them a raise. Isn't that the sort of thing the union objects to?

NOLL:

Well, we do both. . . . We have incentives where they can earn additional dollars if they meet certain standards.

ROONEY:

Labor says there's no sense doing that, because as soon as they attain those standards, you raise the standards.

NOLL:

Oh, I think a lot of that is hogwash. (*Laughs*)

ROONEY:

Does it do workers any good to work harder?

NOLL:

Yes, it does.

ROONEY:

It does *you* good, but does it do *them* good?

NOLL:

Yes, it does. Because it sets a pace and, by and large, the people respect the people that are working in a plant. Don't ever kid yourself that they don't. There's more respect for the people that are working than for the people who are goofing off.

William Winpisinger is the tough, friendly vice-president of the Machinist and Aerospace Workers Union. The day we talked to him, he was tough . . . I was friendly.

ROONEY:

A man named Sanford Noll said that American workers are making so much money they take off whenever they feel like it.

267

WINPISINGER (*laughs*):

I doubt they're even making as much money as he is.

ROONEY:

He was in Fort Lauderdale on vacation when he said that. What do you think about people like Sanford Noll?

WINPISINGER:

Well, it's people like him that make jobs for union officers like myself.

ROONEY:

There are statistics, for instance, in Detroit, and I imagine within your union, of how much more absenteeism there is on a Friday or on a Monday or on a nice summer day.

WINPISINGER:

There are some occupations that seem to develop that statistical base.

ROONEY:

Does a guy have a right to do that? How do you feel as a union person?

WINPISINGER:

Well, I think he has a right not to work if he doesn't want to work, yes.

ROONEY:

Are Americans working as hard as they could or should?

WINPISINGER:

I think so. I've always felt so.

ROONEY:

What do you say to people who say they aren't?

WINPISINGER:

I think the whole context of our times indicates a reduction of manual labor. We don't work as hard as we once did perhaps in terms of what our father might say because of the tremendous automation of industry today that's taken a lot of the manual labor out of work.

* * *

I wonder if that's really true. I doubt it. Almost every
Saturday morning, I know, I set out for the hardware store to
find that magic tool, the one that's finally going to solve all
my problems ... make the grass easy to cut, snow easy to
shovel, gutters easy to clean, wood easy to saw. You know
how it is. Nothing seems to help. And, anyway, if it does and
I do spend ten minutes less doing one thing, at the end of the
day I spend ten minutes more doing something else. In other
words, I don't *work* less. I *do* more.

The notion that the application of invention to labor will
eliminate work is *wrong*. It always seems as though it's about
to, but it never does. You know ... they're going to invent a
machine that'll take your job away. Right?

Well, the fallacy in the idea that science can contribute to permanent unemployment is that built into the idea is the belief that there's a specific amount of work to be done and that when that's accomplished, we'll be all finished with work.

Well, that's crazy. There's an infinite amount of work to be done, and as far as the unemployment question goes, that's one that we don't have to worry about. All the work will *never* be done by man *or* machine. And if it is ever done, it'll take another hundred years to clean up and put the tools away.

An amazing thing happened during the course of doing this research. I'm not a person who is easily convinced he's wrong, but after traveling across the country and visiting more than a hundred factories and other places of business and after seeing a lot of people leaning on their shovels when they should have been shoveling and then hearing people testify that they don't work hard . . . I have still become convinced, to my great surprise, that Americans *are* working their tails off.

I don't know why we're so convinced we aren't working. I think we all rate ourselves maybe against what we can do when we're at our very best, and of course we aren't at our best very often.

The other thing is, and I'm sure of this, I think a lot of that talk is part of the Good Old Days syndrome. You know . . . things aren't as good as they used to be . . . people don't work the way they used to . . . the snow isn't as deep . . . the roses aren't as red.

Our jokes and our talk are about getting out of work but the fact is, not many of us are happy unless we're working hard and getting some satisfaction from it.

Our lives are a lot different when we're at work than when we're at home, and we're at work a lot of our lives . . . so it makes a big difference to our total happiness whether we like our work or not.

ROONEY:

Do you hate your job?

AUTO WORKER:

No. No. Anybody that hates their job, whether they're in here or anyplace else, I think they're just hurting themselves. Because no matter what you're doing in life, you don't have to fall in love with it, but you shouldn't hate it.

ROONEY:

Do you like working?

WORKMAN:

Sure do.

271

ROONEY:
   What is your job?
MAN:
   Hauling rubbish. Cleaning up.
ROONEY:
   A lot of people wouldn't think that was a very good job, but you don't mind.
MAN:
   No, not at all. Not a bit. I can go to work when I get ready and go home when I get ready. If I don't feel like going today, I don't go.
AUTO-PRODUCTION-LINE WORKER:
   Oh, yeah, I like it. There's days I don't like it too . . . but there's days I do. There's worse jobs and better jobs.
ROONEY:
   How do you feel about working? Do you like it or do you hate it or how do you feel?
TIRE WORKER:
   Well, I don't know. I don't mind once I get here. Sometimes it's just hard getting here.
ROONEY:
   How many of those shoes can you pack up in an hour?
WOMAN SHOE PACKER:
   About twenty-five or thirty an hour.
ROONEY:
   Twenty-five or thirty what?
WOMAN:
   There's twelve in a box. Twenty-five or thirty an hour.
ROONEY:
   Twenty-five or thirty boxes?
WOMAN:
   Cases. Yes.
ROONEY:
   That's a lot of shoes.

WOMAN:

Right.

ROONEY:

Do you ever get them in the wrong boxes?

WOMAN:

Not very often.

ROONEY:

You don't get the size eights in the size ten boxes.

WOMAN:

No. You have to watch all your sizes and stuff . . . and make sure that they match up.

ROONEY:

Do you like your work?

WOMAN:

Real well.

ROONEY:

You really like packing shoes?

WOMAN:

I really do. Very well.

Not only did we find an overwhelming number of people who *like* their jobs, but most people find a way to think that *their* job is just a little special, too.

ROONEY (*watching white line being painted*):

It's not a dull job?

STREET PAINTER:

No, not to say the least; not out here with the traffic going by, because you have some pretty close calls sometimes, you know.

ROONEY:

But you get satisfaction from your job?

STREET PAINTER:

Ah, yes, I definitely do. Because what we're building here is something that's going to last for who knows how long—hundreds of years. So, you know, it's like making history, in a way. You know what I mean? You know it's something that's going on right now and people will be able to see years and years from now.

WOMAN AT CLOTHES FACTORY:

Oh, I like my job. (*Laughs*) If I was sewing, I wouldn't like it because I don't like that type of work when you're sitting all the time.

ROONEY (*on street*):

Do you enjoy your work or are you just working for the money?

MAILMAN:

I enjoy talking to people, you know. Actually, I have—

ROONEY:

No, do you enjoy your work?

MAILMAN:

Yeah. I enjoy my work, yeah. I got this Watergate area down there and, you know, different types of people.

ROONEY: (*to trumpet tester*):

Is that a good one?

TRUMPET TESTER:

It better be good 'cause I passed it already.

ROONEY:

Oh, I see. Well, now, you sound to me like a fellow who'd be in here whether you were getting paid or not. In other words, you're pretty wrapped up in your business, aren't you?

TRUMPET TESTER:

This is my life. This I love. I love this.

ROONEY (*at shoe factory*):

How long have you been at that?

SHOE WORKER:

Forty-two years.

ROONEY:

Same job?

SHOE WORKER:

Same job, yes.

ROONEY:

Do you like it?

SHOE WORKER:

Quite well, yes.

ROONEY:

You wouldn't want to do something else?

SHOE WORKER:

I don't believe so.

ROONEY:

You still enjoy it?

SHOE WORKER:

I still do, yes.

ROONEY (*to second shoe worker*):

When did you start?

GIRL (*polishing shoes*):

Two days after I got out of school, in '73.

ROONEY:

You've been doing it ever since.

GIRL:

Yeah.

ROONEY:

How long are you going to do it?

GIRL:

Ah, I don't know, probably quite a while.

ROONEY:

Do you like working?

GIRL:

Yes. It's pretty easy.

ROONEY:

But you wouldn't work if you didn't need the money?

GIRL:

Well, I think I would. It gets kind of boring sitting around all the time. Nothing to do at home. It keeps me busy.

2ND WOMAN at Clothes Factory:

I've been here thirty-eight years 'cause I've enjoyed every minute of it. I just love my work. (*Laughs*) Many of those years were spent at the sewing machine and I like sewing very much. (*Bell rings.*) That's the end of our break. We have to get back to work.

ROONEY:

Well, I don't want to get you fired after thirty-eight years. You'd better get back.

There's a common opinion that production-line work is dull, monotonous and that everyone hates it. That's just not true. Some production-line jobs that *look* dull don't *seem* dull to the people doing them. And then, not everyone wants an interesting job, either. There are people who like the predictability of the production line.

What happens is we all have problems at home we can't cope with, things we don't get done, bills we can't pay, personal relationships we can't handle. For some people those eight hours at work on a repetitive job are like a day in the country. They're away from their problems and the job provides a satisfying little feeling of accomplishment every ten seconds.

There is companionship, and they're not only free from worry while they're there, they're free to daydream because the job doesn't take any thought after the first few thousand times they've done it.

One of the revolutions that has taken place with hardly any of us noticing it is in the matter of wages being paid to people doing undesirable jobs.

Very often unemployment doesn't mean not being able to find work at all. It means not being able to find the kind of job you think you deserve.

It was always assumed that a job that took muscle paid less than one that took brains. That's because there were more people *with* muscle than with brains. These days everyone is getting so much education that there are more dumb jobs to be done than there are dumb people to do them.

For instance, it's easy to find plenty of high-school teachers now but hard to get someone to pick up the garbage . . . so the price for garbagemen goes up while teachers look for work. In New York City, for instance, the average teacher makes $17,000.

A garbageman, on the other hand, can cost the city $25,000 a year.

In relation to dirty jobs and hard work, I couldn't get Marcel Mulberry, the man I'd met on the beach in Fort Lauderdale, out of my mind. I was curious about whether he worked hard himself, so several weeks later I traveled 1,400 miles north to his apple orchard in the Champlain Valley.

I was surprised to find that Mr. Mulberry's regular employees think he's a good boss and that he himself works like a dog.

ROONEY:

What happened to your tan?

MULBERRY:

Well, it kind of disappeared when I got out in the north country here.

ROONEY:

How long do you spend down there in Fort Lauderdale?

MULBERRY:

Just a month.

Rooney:

Is that what you work for, to be able to live a good life like that?

Mulberry:

That's part of it, yes. I don't know. Of course, I've always been interested in agriculture, and producing food for the public has been a great pleasure for me all my life.

Rooney:

You really resent people who don't work hard?

Mulberry:

I guess most people who are in business do. And our crew here, they're all wonderful workers. They really seem to enjoy it and they're good. The regular people are all wonderful at it, but it's really hard to get people today to come out and do this farm work. We get all the local people we can, and it's quite a hard job to get them with the programs we have today, but—

Rooney:

What do you mean, "the programs we have today"?

Mulberry:

Well, lots of people are on unemployment and they don't care about going out and working at jobs like this, and we can't get enough local help to get the crop harvested. It just goes on the ground. A year before last we lost forty thousand boxes. Rotted on the ground.

We found one of the people not picking Mr. Mulberry's apples sitting in the sun not far from where we had originally found Mr. Mulberry on the beach in Florida.

Beachcomber:

I generally work about six months out of the year and the rest I loaf.

ROONEY:

Does six months do it? Do you get enough money in that time?

BEACHCOMBER:

Enough for what I need. Yeah.

ROONEY:

But don't you think that people who have this great drive to do something, to build cars, to make things, have accomplished a lot for this country that you're enjoying?

BEACHCOMBER:

Hmm, yeah.

ROONEY:

You don't feel guilty at all about not contributing much to that?

BEACHCOMBER:

No, I can't say I do. Most of the things that people have and their wants are entirely different from what I want. I think there's entirely too much progress. I think that's why, to be blunt, things are screwed up today as they are, because there's just—things are just moving entirely too fast.

ROONEY:

What sort of things in life called progress have not been good?

BEACHCOMBER:

Look out in the street. The buildings along the beach. All the landmarks in the United States are being covered with condominiums and buildings. It's just destroying it.

ROONEY:

A lot of people are calling what you represent lazy, no-good loafers. Do you resent that?

BEACHCOMBER:

I don't much pay attention to it.

* * *

Who do you admire most or least . . . that young man or self-made Sam Braen? *(Shown walking his two poodles along Fort Lauderdale dock)* Sam is a cement-and-gravel tycoon from New Jersey. We found him walking toward his yacht in Florida.

SAM BRAEN:

I started when I was thirty-eight years old and I owed the bank five hundred dollars and fifteen years later I wound up owning the bank.

ROONEY:

People don't do that anymore?

BRAEN:

Naw. But I worked twenty-four hours a day. It takes something out of you. But when you get older, why, you can relax.

ROONEY:

What's wrong with people today? Why won't they work?

BRAEN:

Well, you know why, 'cause the giveaway program in the United States is too good.

ROONEY:

How did you start? Did you have money when you started? Your family have money?

BRAEN:

Naw. I didn't have two nickels to rub together.

ROONEY:

So you really made it all yourself?

BRAEN:

That's for sure. I bought myself a Ford truck in 1938, and I wound up owning seven hundred big ones . . . forty thousand dollars a throw.

ROONEY:

Who works best? Are there any groups that work better than other groups? Men? Women? Blacks? Whites?

BRAEN:

No. We have a good mixture of everything in our company.

ROONEY:

And they work about the same?

BRAEN:

Oh, sure. Out of the fifteen hundred employees, I would say, we always had at least two or three hundred colored, and they were darn good. They were in our asphalt departments. They came from the Asphalt Layers Union. And every time I went on the job, why, I'd throw them a fifty-dollar bill and say, "Here, boys, when you get too hot with that stuff on your feet''—you know, its three hundred and sixty degrees—''why, buy what you want with it.'' And they were real good workers, believe me.

ROONEY:

So you got along pretty well with your workers?

BRAEN:

Sure. Well, you have to get along, you know. If you can't beat 'em, you join 'em. Otherwise, they rip ya.

ROONEY:

Do you live alone on the boat?

BRAEN:

No. No. Got my wife.

ROONEY: (*on board yacht*):

Do you find people resenting you and people with wealth enough to buy a boat like this?

MRS. BRAEN:

Well, it hasn't been what you would call an obvious resentment, but the feeling is there except for the workers in the yard who showed so much love for the boat. They worked so very, very hard in building her. But we created many jobs for them, too. For the average person who walks up and down the dock, looks at thing like this and says, ''Boy, it must be easy.'' But it's far from easy.

My husband has worked very hard, provided a lot of employment for a lot of people in order to build this boat. And then, when we were building it, we employed a lot of people . . . the electricians, the people that built the engine, all of them, plus the wonderful woodworkers.

ROONEY:

It's almost a public service you're doing, having a boat like this?

BRAEN:

Well, we like to feel that way. Of course, I think it would be very hard for the average citizen to understand that. But very frankly, yes, that's what it amounts to. I'm glad you said it.

Any economic system is supposed to provide a way for dividing the good things on earth so that no one group gets everything and no one group gets nothing.

The traditional enemies in our economy are business and labor. If it's true that the capitalist believes that things work best in an open market where everyone grabs all he can get for himself, then many labor unions are being attracted to that capitalist philosophy, because that's just what they're doing, grabbing all they can get without much thought about where it's coming from.

It's the opinion of most labor leaders that the only way to proceed is as though they were at war: Big Business versus Big Labor. Sometimes it's difficult for an objective observer to be sympathetic to *either* labor or business. They can both be so selfish, ignorant, power-hungry that you can't admire either one of them.

William Winpisinger typifies the labor leader who isn't going to change his views of how things ought to work any quicker than businessmen like Sam Braen or Sanford Noll.

ROONEY:

What changes would you make if you were president of, say, General Motors that would be beneficial to the worker?

WINPISINGER:

I have no idea. It's an area of expertise that I don't have, don't enjoy, and without knowing a good deal more about it than I do, I'd be unable to even make the wildest guess.

ROONEY:

Well, how can you fight these people without knowing what their problems are?

WINPISINGER:

I think, first and foremost, it has to be recognized that a

union is cast in an adversary relationship, which I think is entirely appropriate. It's quite fashionable nowadays for people to go around trying to create schemes to reduce conflict, get the adversary relationship out of labor relations and everything else.

ROONEY:

It's almost as if you're afraid that if you knew all the facts, you couldn't be a good union man?

WINPISINGER:

No, not at all.

ROONEY:

But you didn't want to know anything about management problems?

WINPISINGER:

They're not my problems. I've got plenty of my own, to operate in behalf of the people who employ me. They don't employ me to run factories. They employ me to do a good job as a union officer and I try to do that.

Irving Bluestone is unusual. He's a soft-spoken intellectual who, as a vice-presdient of the United Auto Workers, nonetheless carries a big stick.

ROONEY:

I'm curious about the qualities that make a good union executive. Aren't they the same that make a good management executive?

BLUESTONE:

No, I don't think so. One must remember that the fundamental drive that motivates a manager of business or industry is profit.

ROONEY:

What's the fundamental drive that motivates you?

BLUESTONE:

I think trying to help others and to build a better society.

There's a vast difference between that and the profit motive. I think what we're after, generally, is to improve the quality of work life in many, many different ways.

Most of us are suspicious of the kind of idealism that Irving Bluestone expresses, but I believe him and I also believe that a lot of American businessmen are idealists who are after something other than a buck.

We're all aware of how evil we can be sometimes, how rotten both labor and business often are. Fortunately, though, for all of us, we're still pleased with ourselves when we're virtuous.

ROONEY (*at clock factory*):
Why does a successful businessman like you, Mr. Miller, keep at it? Why do you get up every morning?

MILLER:
I enjoy the work. I enjoy coming to the factory and I've done this for so many years it's a part of me.

ROONEY:
Is your interest primarily in making money or making clocks?

MILLER:
My interest is in making clocks. And when we make clocks, we make people happy.

Jonathan Bainbridge represents a growing movement in this country—a move to get away from it all, to work outside the confines of a structured society and a regular job. Educated and worldly, Jonathan makes his living as a handyman. He lives with his wife, Suzie, and their child in an old barn that he's fixed up into an interesting home.

People like Jonathan Bainbridge are free in a sense many workers aren't. Since he left the security of getting a weekly paycheck for the freedom of working on his own, he answers to no boss but necessity.

ROONEY:

Can you hide from what you have been, what you started being?

JONATHAN:

Yes. I don't know if it's hiding. It's just finding another way of living.

ROONEY:

It looks like pretty hard work, though.

JONATHAN:

Yeah, but it's fun. It's your ideas that you see growing. Everything's organic. And in the city, it was just working, putting in time, and there wasn't much joy in that.

ROONEY:

You go along with that, Suzie?

SUZIE:

Oh, yeah. For sure.

ROONEY:

You really were doing a clockwork job?

JONATHAN:

Yeah. Clockwork in—in uniform with tie and white shirt and so forth. And it got to be too much.

ROONEY:

What was that job?

JONATHAN:

I was with Delta Airlines.

ROONEY:

And what were you doing?

JONATHAN:

I was a ticket agent at the airport, at Kennedy Airport.

ROONEY:

And how about the good ways of life, though, aside from your psyche. Have you had enough to eat?

JONATHAN:

Oh, yes. Yes. We do a large garden.

ROONEY:

  I notice you drinking beer. You don't grow that, though.

JONATHAN:

  No. No. When the money's coming in, there's enough beer. And as the money doubles, it goes out just as swiftly.

ROONEY:

  Do you have any fears?

JONATHAN:

  It's the same trip that it was in the city. You know? There isn't an escape. As things progress, there are going to be more wants and more desires for acquisitions.

ROONEY:

  In other words, you notice some of the same things happening to you that happened to you in the city?

JONATHAN:

  Yes. Very definitely. As a matter of fact, we have just received a loan to buy a new car. Now maybe that's our diploma. You know, we're back in the mainstream. It sort of felt that way. Whether it's for the better or the worse, I don't know.

Jonathan and Suzie Bainbridge may not be typical. Very few of the people who choose to work outside the system are typical of anything.

FRED STETTNER (*with horse at the Stettner farm*):

  Here, Scarlet, come here.

ROONEY (*aside*):

  For fifteen years, Fred Stettner worked in an office in New York City.

ROONEY:

  How much did you know about horses in the beginning?

FRED:

  Nothing.

ROONEY:
  You didn't?
FRED:
  Not a thing.
ROONEY:
  You mean, you never grew up with horses at all?
FRED:
  No. I grew up in the city.
ROONEY (*aside*):
  Today he's working a lot harder for a lot less money and

291

loving it. Seven years ago Fred and his wife, Enid, and their three children moved into this old farmhouse on a two-lane blacktop road three miles from a couple of towns in upstate New York you never heard of.

ROONEY:

And what were you trying to get away from?

FRED:

I would say the difficulty of living in the city ... the problems that one has living in the city and raising children ... a desire for a better kind of freer existence, I think, which you can find in a place like this.

ROONEY:

I have this theory that the same thing keeps happening to the same people. Doesn't the same thing happen to you as a couple here as it did in New York City?

ENID:

No. I don't think it does, because here we have something to work for together and we didn't in New York.

ROONEY:

What would happen if vast numbers of Americans decided to quit the production line at General Motors and find themselves a house out in the middle of nowhere and grow some things and keep some animals?

ENID:

Well, probably we wouldn't need as many cars. The value system would be totally different. It's a very different value system. We work so that we can live the life that we want. It's not just to accumulate goods.

FRED:

Although somehow we have accumulated a lot.

ENID (*laughs*):

We happen to have accumulated a lot of things. I find that people who are most interested in doing what we do are people who are in very high-pressure jobs.

ROONEY:

I look around at what you have here and I notice tremendous pressure. You had a kid you had to pick up from school and rush to some musical rehearsal thing.

ENID:

Right.

ROONEY:

You've got a house that needs cleaning. The dishes are in the sink...you haven't done them yet. You've got problems. You've got to go to town tomorrow. You've got a library meeting. I think you're still under pressure.

ENID:

We didn't say we weren't.

FRED:

But our lives won't fall apart if we don't do all these things.

ENID:

It's pressure that we don't mind. We enjoy this pressure. There's so much to do now. We are always busy. We are always doing something. But it's things that are meaningful to us. It's not imposed from the outside. It's imposed from within.

FRED:

I think that to work at something and do something that you're not really particularly interested in your whole life, just to wait until you're able to collect your Social Security and your pension, is...you miss the whole point.

The Stettners and the Bainbridges may live happily ever after where they are, but they'll always be city people living in the country. George LaPelle never lived anywhere but the country. George works around a lake where many people have vacation homes and he's exactly what the whole world needs...someone to take *care* of things.

There's nothing George can't do. Although there are a lot

of things he *won't* do if he doesn't feel like it. We talked to him one day he didn't feel like it.

ROONEY:

What's that going to cost somebody to get a job like that done?

LAPELLE:

You want me to quote you a price?

ROONEY:

Not me. I don't have to pay for it.

LAPELLE:

I don't know. As I say, you don't know till you get down there and see what's gone underneath.

ROONEY:

You're pretty cagey about what it's going to cost somebody.

LAPELLE:

Well, certainly. I wouldn't tell you how much it's going to cost you.

ROONEY:

About how many hours do you put in a day?

LAPELLE:

Eight.

ROONEY:

Are you careful about that?

LAPELLE:

Careful? No, if I've got something else to do, I do eight here and maybe another four at home.

ROONEY:

You'd make more money if you worked nine hours, wouldn't you?

LAPELLE:

What am I going to with the money?

ROONEY:

Spend it, I suppose.

LaPelle:

Pay taxes on it.

Rooney:

If you had your choice in the whole world, what would you be doing?

LaPelle:

Probably what I'm doing now.

Rooney:

You like it about as much as anything you can think of.

LaPelle:

Well, I certainly wouldn't be a politician.

Rooney:

What satisfactions do you get out of work? I mean, what is it you like about it?

LaPelle:

Well, you accomplish a little something. Fix people up a place to live or something.

Rooney:

You like that?

LaPelle:

Sure.

Rooney:

If you had a million dollars, what would you do?

LaPelle:

I don't know. You get me a million dollars and I'll let you know afterwards.

Rooney:

Do you think you'd keep doing what you're doing?

LaPelle:

Oh, I'd do something, sure. I'd have to do something.

Rooney:

You've got a pretty nice house here?

LaPelle:

I've done all the work myself. Otherwise I wouldn't have it.

Rooney:

You've got two cars—a truck and a car.

LaPelle:

Yeah.

Rooney:

No worries.

LaPelle:

What do you mean, no worries? I've got everybody *else's* worries.

Rooney:

That's pretty much what you are, isn't it? When that phone rings, it's someone else's worry?

LAPELLE:

Yeah, that's about what it boils down to.

ROONEY:

What's a typical phone call you're apt to get late at night?

LAPELLE:

Oh, somebody's furnace don't run or somebody's water pump quit or their washing machine's bothering or something like that. Usually, you just plug 'em in or something and they start working.

ROONEY:

What about young people? Do you think young people are working as hard as they used to?

LAPELLE:

Most of them don't work at all.

ROONEY:

Why's that, do you think?

LAPELLE *(laughs):*

Too much education.

ROONEY:

You think people who are more educated work less hard?

LAPELLE:

Oh, sure.

ROONEY:

There are some pretty nice places down on the lake. Do you ever get hating the people who own them?

LAPELLE:

No. Why should I?

ROONEY:

People with boats and a lot of money who don't look as though they work very hard?

LAPELLE:

Well, that could include you, but you don't bother me too much.

* * *

As I understand it, and, of course, I may not understand it, if you're a capitalist, you believe in free enterprise. And what that means is, you think that if you work as hard as you can to get as much as you can for yourself, you'll be better off and so will everyone else.

If you build a factory and make a million dollars, you don't have to feel guilty about being rich; you can feel good about it, because in the process of making that million dollars, you've put 350 people to work in *your* factory.

The other extreme, socialism, is based on the idea that no one should get rich *or* poor. All the people should own all the businesses and the workers divide up the profits.

Socialism and capitalism seem to be living side by side in this country.

A lot of working people buy stock in the company they work for. The workers' pension funds are investing so much that within the next ten years they'll own a majority of the stock in all American corporations. Then who do the workers strike against?

So it's no longer a question of capitalism or socialism. Capitalism is taking socialism in as a business partner.

SWITCHBOARD OPERATOR:
Lincoln Electric.

The Lincoln Electric Company in Cleveland makes half a dozen products that are too dull to tell you about unless you're an arc welder. But the Lincoln Electric Company itself is one of the most interesting in the whole country. They're very suspicious of reporters and cameramen, but we did get in.

They aren't making any top-secret weapons. What they're guarding so jealously is not any mysterious manufacturing process, either. It's their incredible record of success. They

just don't want anything, including a lot of talk about it on
television, to disturb it.

The company has the best worker-participation plan in the
United States. No music. No swimming pool. No bowling
alleys. No tricks. Just money.

ROONEY:

Is it any secret what you make at Lincoln Electric?

1ST WORKER:

Without the bonus, I'd say probably the average is ten to
twelve thousand dollars a year.

ROONEY:

And what would the bonus be?

1ST WORKER:

Well, it'd probably be somewhere, roughly, just about 90
percent of that.

ROONEY:

In other words, you could make around twenty thousand
dollars. . . .

1ST WORKER:

I think the average guy's probably making close to that.

ROONEY:

I guess that's why they want to work at Lincoln Electric?

1ST WORKER:

That's why they want to work here, right.

2ND WORKER:

Everybody makes pretty good money here. You enjoy it,
you know. You enjoy some of the finer things in life. You
know, some things that you probably would never have a
chance to working someplace else.

ROONEY:

You mean, you're more apt to have two cars in your family
than the average worker?

2ND WORKER:

More apt to, probably. More apt to take a vacation. More apt to have a savings account. Whereas, I suppose a lot of people don't have that nowadays, with the economy being what it is.

They do a lot of things differently at Lincoln and it's all directed toward increasing productivity. Most workers do more than one job. Some do a whole series of jobs that would keep ten men busy a lot of places.

By their own choice, the men work in a plant that's dingy, dark and it isn't air-conditioned. To make any changes would cost money . . . the workers' *own* money.

The offices where the paperwork for this multimillion-dollar-a-year operation is done at Lincoln Electric aren't much better. Most of the staff works in one large room and the manager is thrown in there with them.

All promotions at Lincoln Electric are made from within the company. Not some of them—*all* of them—and they're made on ability, not seniority. They don't end up with a lot of duds in high places because they've been there a long time.

There are no little coffeepots or transistor radios around here either. Each worker is rated every six months on four factors. His bonus depends on his ratings. Since 1934, the total bonus paid equals the total wages . . . and the wages are pretty good. No one at Lincoln Electric has been laid off since 1958. The workers are nonunion and have no interest in joining one.

ROONEY:

Is it a form of socialism?

1ST WORKER:

Oh, I wouldn't say it was a form of socialism. I would say it's more like a dictatorship in the fact that the heads of the company completely run it. But it's not a dictatorship, you

know, in the fact that the men do have the freedom to have
things changed. We have an advisory board. We can have
things changed when we feel we need change, and that's
one of the nice things, where you can talk with an official
of the company.

ROONEY:

Like what? Give me an example.

1ST WORKER:

Well, a couple of weeks ago, I had a production problem
on the line. I couldn't get it solved through the regular
channels in the shop, so I went up and saw the president of
the company.

ROONEY:

You just went in?

1ST WORKER:

I made a phone call and asked him if I could come in
and see him, and he was glad to see me and I went up and
talked to him, and he solved the problem and now we're
running smooth again.

ROONEY:

You couldn't do that in many companies.

1ST WORKER:

I don't think you could do this in many factories. I worked
for other companies that you couldn't even get to see the
president to say good morning to him, let alone talk out the
problems and get them solved.

3RD WORKER:

If you're going to have to get up at five-thirty in the
morning, it's a good place to come.

ROONEY:

What's different about Lincoln Electric?

3RD WORKER:

Well, Lincoln Electric, as far as a manufacturer, is probably
a perfect form of capitalism.

ROONEY:

Is it capitalism or is it socialism?

3RD WORKER:

No. It's capitalism. Look at the wages we make. It's strictly you get paid for what you do. And if General Motors would do that, we'd be able to buy new Eldorados for six thousand dollars.

The Donnelly Mirror Company in Holland, Michigan, has had a profit-sharing system called the Scanlon Plan for twenty years now. The Scanlon Plan, a watered-down version of Lincoln Electric's program, is the most widely used profit-sharing plan in the country.

Productivity at Donnelly is good, absenteeism rare and the workers seem to like it.

WOMAN WORKER:

I enjoy coming here, working with the girls. We have a real good time, a real good group.

It's hard for an observer to know when a profit-sharing plan is a superficial trick of management to get more production out of workers and when it's a genuine plan to benefit both workers *and* management.

Dick Arthur is an articulate middleman who makes his living as an industry consultant selling the Scanlon Plan to both management and labor.

ROONEY:

Are all these plans bringing us closer towards socialism in America?

DICK ARTHUR:

Just the opposite. I think America has had a tendency to go in the socialistic direction. The thing that we're teaching is probably the purest form of capitalism that could ever exist. Because we're in effect saying, "Hey, you want to share the loot, then produce. Either work harder or work smarter and you're going to get your share. And, incidentally, when you get your share, you're going to make me more, and you don't mind making me rich if I'm making you rich at the same time, do you?" And you say, "Hell, no, as long as I'm getting mine, too." For example, if they've been averaging 10 percent on sales we put our plan in and say, "Okay, from now on everything that you make over 10 percent, we're going to split fifty/fifty."

ROONEY:

William Winpisinger, the union official we talked to, said: "What's this everything over 10 percent? Why not start fifty-fifty from the beginning?"

ARTHUR:

First place, you can't get an honest-to-God capitalist to do it, so why waste your time talking about it? Second, it's impractical. As a matter of fact, one of the things that we get really turned on about this whole program is that it's a tremendous educational process for people. They have to understand that the money doesn't fall down from trees...that it costs money to build buildings, to buy equipment, to buy tools, and a company has to be making a fair profit. And I say, "Well, okay, what the hell *is* fair?" If I can put my money in a bank and earn 5 percent and sit with my feet on a footstool, certainly 10 percent working my tail off is not exorbitant. And so there has to be a creaming of the profits, so to speak, for the company.

ROONEY:

You used the phrase "an honest-to-God capitalist." Who's harder to educate...that honest-to-God capitalist or the hardheaded union official?

ARTHUR:

My own personal experience is it's the capitalist. Okay. But I think there's a reason. Perhaps you could even justify it.

Here you have a man that has put his money into a company. It's *his* money. It's *his* investment. And so when you start saying to him, "Hey, look, we want you to share some of the fruits of your investment," he's hearing you from a different point of view. Where a union official will say, "What the hell, the more the merrier. You know, the more the troops get the better I can look, so why should we fight it?" We do have union leaders who do resist it sometimes but primarily because they see it as a threat to their little kingdom.

We go into a plant where they've had a union and they've had it for maybe thirty years, and we get union and management together, and we say, "Look, for the last thirty years, management has exerted a tremendous amount of energy in how to screw the union, the union has worked overtime figuring how to screw management and in the meantime we're faced with world competition, and I say let's all get together and screw the French."

And to me, this is capitalism at its best . . . free enterprise at its best.

There's something in the American character that likes to fool itself. When a worker participates in profits, that's a form of socialism, not capitalism. Americans fool themselves a thousand ways, and they often end up believing what is simply not true.

For instance, no matter how much it amuses us to think we're goofing off, and in spite of the evidence that in some places we obviously are, the hard fact is that, man for man, woman for woman, machine for machine, we're producing more than anyone in the world.

We're producing 35 percent more than the Germans, 64 percent more than the Japanese, and 85 percent more than the British. These are not opinions, they're statistics.

I found out four things that surprised me during the course of assembling this report.

First, Americans are working hard even though it often seems as though they are not.

WORKER:
Well, I can speak for my crew. We work pretty hard, I think.

Second, people like their jobs even though they often talk as though they do not.

WORKER:

You hear some people complaining, but I can't see where they should. I think they should enjoy their work.

Third, workers don't hate the boss and they don't resent the money he makes, either. They'd rather have him drive a Cadillac than a Volkswagen.

WORKER:

If it wasn't for these people, I wouldn't have a job. Right?

Fourth, and this was the biggest surprise of all to me, we're becoming a socialist nation within the framework of our free-enterprise system . . . whether anyone likes it or not.

If I'm wrong, I'm sure you won't hesitate to correct me.

UGLY

For a long time now a lot of us have excused ourselves for not knowing what is ugly and what is beautiful by saying to someone who does "That's what you think" or "Every man is entitled to his own opinion."

We set out to see whether it's true that everyone has a right to his own opinion. We wanted to find out whether beauty and ugliness are qualities of their own, independent of the person who looks at them.

Standards of beauty are set by those who know most about a subject. If other people who don't know as much about it see no beauty, we ought to be able to say they are wrong.

There are some subjects about which we all consider ourselves expert. What about standards of ugly, though? Who says what is ugly and what isn't . . . and for what reasons do they say it?

One of the disconcerting characteristics of ugly is that so many of us agree about *what* it is without being able to say *why* it is.

For instance, junk in any form strikes us all as offensive to the eye and ugly. America the beautiful may actually lead the world in ugly, and it seems to be because we have so much to throw away. Anything discarded is ugly. We make more cars, so we throw more away . . . and we are running out of ugly places to throw them, so we throw them anywhere and make *that* place ugly. Garbage or anything that has anything to do with garbage is ugly, and because garbage is a by-product of affluence, we have lots of it.

One of the things that seem to be true about ugly is that it is often associated with deterioration. Anything that doesn't look as good as it used to is on the way to becoming ugly. It is probably because anything that doesn't look as good as it used to is growing older and reminds us of ourselves and of death.

This idea, if it's true at all, doesn't account for everything ugly, though, because that factor is not always present. It is possible to make brand-new junk that is ugly. Not only that, but a lot of things which look good in their own place become ugly-looking someplace else. The object, itself unchanged, is changed by your reaction to it.

A woman's hair can be a thing of great beauty, one of her most attractive physical attributes. We are agreed. Now envision a well-set dinner table, with silverware, and candlelight. The soup is served. And this is the strange thing about ugly . . . take just one of the beautiful hairs from the woman's head and put it in the soup and both the hair and the soup are repulsive.

Almost anything out of place, anything that is not where it was meant to be, strikes us as ugly. Virgin snow in a country setting is beautiful. It is attractive on a ski slope. It can even

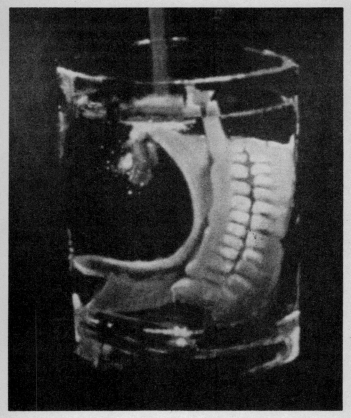

be beautiful, freshly fallen, on a city. But in the city, snow quickly becomes used, out of place, dirty, dying . . . and ugly.

A smile is attractive and white teeth in a good mouth are beautiful. Take the teeth out of their natural setting and they are not beautiful, they are ugly . . . even when they're smiling. Teeth in a glass have about them several of the attributes we associate with ugly. They represent an object out of place and they also suggest the losing battle we are all fighting against deterioration.

Life is beautiful.

Death is ugly.

It is always assumed that an interest in the beauty of Nature is a sign of goodness in a person. It is a strange assumption we make and neither do we understand why, generally speaking, we consider Nature to be beautiful.

Man is more apt to see beauty in symmetry and ugliness in disorder. Nature, superficially at least, appears to be disorderly. Left alone with Nature, man starts to rearrange what he finds there. He proceeds quite often with some principle of equation in his mind. He is driven by the notion that if he puts something on one side of anything, he ought to put another thing just like it on the other side. Then he calls it beautiful.

Symmetry is probably beautiful to a lot of us because we see in its design a clear plan. It suggests we can arrange and control our world . . . that we are not wet leaves in a stream of water. Our reaction to it is therefore pleasant and we call it beautiful.

There are further complications to this business of ugly which we do not completely understand. We would all agree that this abandoned gas station is ugly. No one has a single formula for ugly that fits every case, but the gas station has about it a good many of the characteristics which would be included in anyone's definition.

We have enlarged and framed one piece of the film showing the station. To our untrained eye it looks as artful as many pictures we have seen hanging in galleries. But if the gas station is ugly, is this a work of art and therefore beautiful?

And one hard question leads to another. If a scene that we all agree is ugly is graphically and accurately represented on canvas in oil paint, can *it* then be properly called a work of art and therefore beautiful?

There is a wide variety to ugliness. There are ugly things, ugly sounds, ugly people . . . and even motion can be ugly.

There is often something about movement that can suggest the thing is not working the way it ought to and this lack of grace is ugly. We all find grace and beauty in the purposeful design of a sailboat. Everything about how it has been made improves its ability to be pushed swiftly through the water by the wind. It is an object of beauty, doing what it does best. Another boat, perhaps as well built but in another situation and another condition and no longer doing what it can do, is not beautiful. Rotting in the mud at low tide, it is an eyesore.

There is grace in the design of the *Queen Mary* . . . but the ultimately purposeful tugboats that push her and pull her . . . are they ugly or are they beautiful?

Why then do we find the hippopotamus, whose shape is as ideal as the trotting horse or the sailboat for doing what it does—wallowing in the mud—why do we find the hippopotamus one of the ugliest animals on earth?

And if we are repulsed by the hippopotamus, why are we attracted to elephants . . . or repelled by the grace of a snake?

Why is an alligator in a swamp ugly and repulsive . . . but an item of high fashion as a pocketbook on Fifth Avenue?

And what about man's closest relative in the animal kingdom, the ape? We're generally agreed he's ugly . . . but why are we agreed?

THE FACES OF CHRIST

Tomorrow is Christmas. It is the day Christians celebrate the birth of Jesus Christ, the Hebrew prophet they believe to have been the Son of God. Although Christ's teaching and his apparent goodness would seem to transcend the significance of what he looked like, almost a hundred generations of Christians have wanted some image toward which to direct their worship.

One of the difficulties in providing visualization of Christ is that no artist who lived when Christ lived drew any likeness of him that exists today. Neither was any physical description of Christ provided in the Bible.

Because the early Christian movement was disapproved of by public officials, Christ's followers used symbolic representations to conceal their affiliation. In an early church council these and other symbols were disapproved, and it was decreed that from that time onward Christ would be portrayed as a man.

The first efforts to picture Christ seem to have been Byzantine, meaning done in the city of Byzantium, the

Turkish capital, once Constantinople, now called Istanbul. Many of them were mosaics, done in the third and fourth centuries. Christ was also frequently portrayed on the walls of the crypts in Roman cemeteries of that period.

The Old Testament Book of Isaiah says of the coming Messiah, "He was devoid of beauty and a sufferer."

Many of the earliest artists formed their concept of Jesus from this comment. A historian named Tertullian, who lived in the year 200, said of him, "There was nothing outstanding about Christ's flesh, and it was just this contrast with his personality which struck everyone. Far from emanating Divine radiance, his body had not even simple human beauty. The passion and the humility he suffered left their mark, and it was deprived of all charm by his suffering."

Neither lay nor theological historians have been able to reconstruct any chronological order to most of the events in Christ's life. Although nothing at all is known of him for more than thirty of his thirty-five years, Renaissance artists were prolific in portraying the infant and child Jesus. Some of the world's most treasured artworks are those of Christ with his mother.

As the Christian movement spread and missionaries told the story, artists around the world painted the Jesus Christ they saw in their own mind. To the Christians of the Far East, he was Oriental; to the Indians, Indian; to the Africans, he was black—and who is to say otherwise if they see him so?

It is probable that if Christ had been born Roman or Greek, contemporary likenesses of him would have been painted or chiseled in stone.

The sophistication of modern religious belief, where there is any at all, prohibits a literal visualization of the idea of Jesus Christ. A picture of God as a bearded and benign elderly gentleman in a flowing robe is unacceptable now even to the true believer. As a result, Christ seldom inspires the imagination of the modern artist; and where he does, the image he paints is not apt to evoke much reverence. Skepticism has dissolved the pigment on the canvas, leaving in its place a blurred image. An artist, painting without a subject, illustrates his *own* state of mind.

The only description of Christ ever found purporting to have been written by a contemporary is not generally accepted as authentic, but it has been the basis of many great works of art. It was said to have been written by a public official in Jerusalem during Christ's lifetime. ''There has appeared here in our time a man of great power named Jesus Christ. The people call him a prophet of truth, and his disciples the Son of God. He raises the dead and cures the sick. He is in stature a man of middle height and well-proportioned. He has a venerable face. His hair is the color of ripe chestnuts—smooth almost to the ears, but above them waving and curling, with a slight bluish radiancy, and it flows over his shoulders. It is parted in the middle on the top of his head after the fashion of the people of Nazareth. His brow is smooth and very calm, with a face without a wrinkle or a blemish, lightly tinged with red. His nose and mouth are faultless. His beard is luxuriant and uncreased, of the same color as his hair—not long, but parted at the chin. His countenance is full of simplicity and love. His eyes are expressive and brilliant. He is terrible in reproof, sweet and gentle in admonition, cheerful without ceasing to be grave. His figure is slender and erect. His hands and arms are beautiful to see. He is the fairest of the children of men.''

Belief is a quality of its own. It is a virtue independent of that which is believed in. ''The Christ head, the Christ face, what man will ever paint, chisel or carve it?'' Carl Sandburg asked. ''When finished, it would float and gleam, cry and laugh with every face born human. And how,'' the poet asked, ''can you crowd all the tragic and comic faces of mankind into one face?''

By the year 2000, 2 out of 3 Americans could be illiterate.

It's true.

Today, 75 million adults… about one American in three, can't read adequately. And by the year 2000, U.S. News & World Report envisions an America with a literacy rate of only 30%.

Before that America comes to be, you can stop it… by joining the fight against illiteracy today.

Call the Coalition for Literacy at toll-free **1-800-228-8813** and volunteer.

Volunteer Against Illiteracy. The only degree you need is a degree of caring.

Ad Council   Coalition for Literacy

Warner Books is proud to be an active supporter of the Coalition for Literacy.